BOTH SIDES FACE EAST

EDITED BY
Julia Sushytska, ariel rosé,
& Alisa Slaughter

VOLUME 1: Durable Words

Boston
2025

Library of Congress Cataloging-in-Publication Data

Names: Sushytska, Julia, 1978- editor | rosé, ariel, 1982- editor | Slaughter, Alisa editor
Title: Both sides face east / edited by Julia Sushytska, ariel rosé, and Alisa Slaughter.
Description: Boston : Academic Studies Press, 2025- | Includes bibliographical references. | Contents: v. 1. Durable words
Identifiers: LCCN 2024061781 (print) | LCCN 2024061782 (ebook) | ISBN 9798887197401 v. 1 hardback | ISBN 9798887197418 v. 1 adobe pdf | ISBN 9798887197425 v. 1 epub
Subjects: LCSH: War--Literary collections | LCGFT: Poetry | Short stories
Classification: LCC PN6071.W35 B68 2025 (print) | LCC PN6071.W35 (ebook) | DDC 808.8/03581--dc23/eng/20250220
LC record available at https://lccn.loc.gov/2024061781
LC ebook record available at https://lccn.loc.gov/2024061782

ISBN 9798887197401 v. 1 hardback
ISBN 9798897830299 v. 1 paperback
ISBN 9798887197418 v. 1 adobe pdf
ISBN 9798887197425 v. 1 ePub

Book design by PHi Business Solutions
Cover design by Mari Kynovich

Original artwork (oil on canvas) by Oleh Panasiuk, reproduced by permission.

Published by Academic Studies Press
1007 Chestnut Street
Newton, MA 02464, USA
press@academicstudiespress.com
www.academicstudiespress.com

Fondation
Jan Michalski

Contents

Translators

Céline Anger, Gábor Danyi, Garrett Howard, Roman Ivashkiv, Sabrina Jaszi, Andriy Lysenko, Philip Nikolayev, ariel rosé, Marco Schindelmann, Ena Selimović, Zsuzsa Selyem, Marci Shore, Alisa Slaughter, Julia Sushytska, Gabriele Tiemann, Frank L. Vigoda

Foreword

Uilleam Blacker

Most wars are fought over territory. Historical and cultural arguments are invoked in order to prove 'rightful' ownership, as are more pragmatic arguments about national security, about self defense against purported threats. These can be reasonable, based in fact and reality, or they can be invented, disingenuous, vexatious; either way, they often hide other goals, such as the protection of wealth and power, the seizure of resources, the facilitation of political domination. All these things play out in struggles over the contours of a border, over the control of areas of land.

The war zone is imagined as abstract chunks of territory, as lines and points on maps. Those waging wars (and also those observing and analyzing them from afar) ignore the fact that these places are messy, rich, meaningful landscapes in which real people live; they ignore the fact that every maneuver, every raid, every strike affects human beings, their livelihoods, homes, and environments. Those who have lived through war understand this clash between the blind merciless-ness of abstraction and the fragility of living communities. They understand the contingency of borders and the persistence of connection to place. The writers who emerge from war-afflicted societies also understand these things. Their imagined landscape is deeper than any general's map, even if it may not be marked out on official maps. They are sensitive to each wound in the soil and the bricks. "I'd like to tell you that the land here has not changed one bit," writes Iya Kiva, "but that would be untrue, the kind of cruel and futile lie / that they sprinkle to soothe a child's eager curiosity." Writers from these places know that lost homes may have to live on only in words—in their words, which makes their task all the more urgent. "Once you've left your home, words cannot be found for the love / of a place where you'll relapse into the silent corridor of childhood," writes Kiva. Yes, perhaps the task is difficult or even impossible, perhaps language is just not equal to loss. In that case, we must, as Kiva does here, be able to speak at least about that strange space of disorientation as much as we speak of the rooms, streets and fields where our pre-war selves still dwell.

I see an attempt on the part of the writers presented in this book to orientate themselves and us in the real territory of war. Their project is an alternative to a map. I find it inspiring and life-giving. Each text in this volume is a small gesture of true presence (even if it speaks of absence), an act of deep verticality in a world of lethally flat maps. Such writing cannot reclaim the physical territory from the tanks, only the Armed Forces of Ukraine can do that; but texts can act on the geography of the tired imagination and the beleaguered soul, turning ravaged and abandoned space into loved, protected place.

September 2, 2024

Переднє слово

Віллем Блекер

Більшість воєн точиться за територію. Аргументи з царини історії, культури, національної безпеки і самозахисту від ймовірних загроз наводяться для того, щоб довести «законність» володіння. Вони можуть бути обґрунтованими, заснованими на фактах і реальності, а можуть бути вигаданими, нещирими, дратівливими; в будь-якому випадку, за ними здебільшого ховаються інші цілі, такі як захист багатства і влади, загарбання ресурсів, сприяння політичному домінуванню. Усе це проявляється в боротьбі за контури кордону, за контроль над ділянками землі.

Зони воєнних дій уявляються як абстрактні шматки території, як лінії і точки на мапах. Ті, хто веде війну (а також ті, хто спостерігає і аналізує її здалеку), ігнорують той факт, що ці місця є насиченими значеннями ландшафтами, замешканими реальними людьми. Вони ігнорують той факт, що кожен маневр, кожен рейд, кожен удар торкається людей, їхніх засобів до існування, домівок, навколишнього середовища. Ті, хто пережив війну, розуміють це зіткнення між сліпою нещадністю абстракції і крихкістю живих спільнот. Вони розуміють мінливість кордонів і незмінність зв'язку з місцем. Письменники, які походять з постраждалих від війни суспільств, також це розуміють. Їхній уявний ландшафт, навіть якщо він не позначений на жодній офіційній мапі, глибший за будь-яку генеральську мапу. Вони чутливі до кожної рани землі та цегли.

«Я хотіла б тобі сказати, що земля тут анітрошечки не змінилася, — пише Ія Ківа, — але це буде неправда, це буде жорстока даремна брехня, / якою притрушують цупку дитячу цікавість». Письменники з цих місць знають, що, можливо, втрачені домівки продовжують своє життя лише у словах — у їхніх словах, що робить їхнє завдання ще більш нагальним. «Раз полишивши дім — не відшукати слів для любові / до місця, в якому впадеш у дитинства глухий коридор», — пише Ківа. Так, можливо, це завдання складне, ба навіть неможливе, можливо мова просто не в змозі опанувати втрату. У такому разі нам, услід за Ією, належить навчитись говорити бодай про цей дивний простір дезорієнтації так само, як ми говоримо про кімнати, вулиці та лани, де все ще живуть наші довоєнні «я».

Я бачу спробу представлених у цій книжці авторів зорієнтувати себе і нас на реальній території війни. Їхній проект — це альтернатива мапі. Я знаходжу його надихаючим і життєдайним. Кожен текст у цій книжці — це маленький жест справжньої присутності (навіть якщо він розповідає про відсутність), акт рішучої вертикалізації у світі смертельно пласких мап. Таке письмо не може відвоювати фізичну територію у танків, це під силу лише ЗСУ, але тексти здатні впливати на географію втомленої уяви та обложеної душі, перетворюючи спустошений і покинутий простір на любе, затишне місце.

2 вересня 2024

Translated by Andriy Lysenko

Foreword to *Durable Words*

Jessica Berlin

War destroys what should endure. Sovereign borders, bustling cities, human bodies violated and broken. Yet the most enduring symbols that have emerged from Russia's war against Ukraine aren't images of violence, but words. Simple, short, and fearless:

президент тут. ми всі тут. *The President is here. We are all here.*

Русский военный корабль, иди на хуй. *Russian warship, go fuck yourself.*

слава україні. *Slava Ukraïni. Glory to Ukraine.*

These words have become international symbols of Ukrainian courage under fire. Their power, however, lies not only in their reflection of the speakers' courage. They echo with over three hundred years of bravery and sacrifice, as generation after generation of Ukrainians have stood against imperialists trying to destroy their nation, people, culture and language. Generations of murdered writers and language bans later, Ukrainians' words today ring out that much louder, uniting and inspiring people across the world connected by the shared will to live free, in peace.

The writers featured in this volume come from diverse backgrounds but share that common will. They challenge histories and identities, reminding the world, themselves, and each other who they are and what is worth fighting for. They ask difficult questions that don't always have answers. In a proud cacophony of perspectives, languages, and styles, they share a common truth: we are all here. Our people survive. We won't be silenced.

Words carry the power of memory and spirit. For oppression to succeed, it must break the memory and spirit of a people; therefore, oppressors seek to silence the oppressed. In that small transitive equation, we glimpse the path to victory: never shut up. So long as we continue to shout and write and debate our truth, the oppressors have failed. Our words will endure, to someday guide and inspire future generations as words from the past have inspired us.

August 30, 2024

Передмова до «Довічних слів»

Джессіка Берлін

Війна руйнує, нівечить та ламає те, що має зберегтись. Суверенні кордони, галасливі міста, людські тіла. Однак, в результаті війни Росії проти України постало й дещо незнищенне. Не образи насильства, а слова. Прості, короткі та безстрашні:

Ми всі тут.
Російський військовий корабель, йди на хуй.
Слава Україні.

Ці слова стали міжнародним символом української мужності під вогнем. Однак їхня сила полягає не лише в тому, що вони відображають мужність тих, хто їх виголошує. Вони перегукуються з більш ніж трьохсотрічною історією хоробрості та жертовності, коли покоління за поколінням українці протистояли імперіалістам, які намагалися знищити їхню націю, народ, культуру та мову. Минуло кілька генерацій вбитих письменників і численних заборон рідної мови. Сьогодні слова українців звучать набагато гучніше, об'єднуючи і надихаючи людей по всьому світу. Об'єднуючи прагненням жити вільно, в мирі та злагоді.

Представлені у цій збірці письменники походять з різних країв, але їх об'єднує спільна воля. Вони кидають виклик історії та ідентичностям, нагадуючи світові, собі та один одному, хто вони є і за що варто боротися. Вони ставлять складні питання, на які не завжди є відповіді. У гордій поліфонії поглядів, мов і стилів вони поділяють спільну істину: ми всі тут. Наші народи живі. Нас не змусять замовкнути.

Слова несуть у собі силу пам'яті і духу. Аби досягнути власних цілей, гнобителі мають зламати пам'ять і дух народу; тому то вони й прагнуть змусити пригноблених замовкнути. А, значить, шлях до перемоги над гнобителями один: ніколи не мовчати. Допоки ми продовжуємо кричати, писати і дискутувати про те, що є істиною, гноблення зазнає краху. Наші слова вистоять, щоб колись спрямовувати і надихати майбутні покоління, як надихають слова з минулого нас.

30 серпня 2024

Translated by Andriy Lysenko

From the Editors

Soon after Russia's full-scale invasion of Ukraine, in February 2022, Julia Sushytska organized a series of online panels at Occidental University in Los Angeles, California. The conversations and relationships that ensued prompted the three of us to propose a combination online and in-person symposium held in Lviv, Ukraine, in June and July 2023. Many of the writers included in this volume took part in the Lviv and/or Los Angeles gatherings, and the organizers realized that the ephemeral nature of conversation also called for a record and a synthesis, an acknowledgment that some of the ideas and creations of this time will endure. We committed to three principles: a focus on Ukrainian writers, anti-imperialism in the broadest possible definition, and abundant translation. The latter was an important response to the inevitable "international English" lingua franca of much academic and artistic discourse, incomplete and imperfect as our efforts might be.

We want to take this opportunity to present our own thoughts about the symposium and the current moment, as well as introduce the next two volumes. *Both Sides Face East: Borders de Todos Lados* will feature international writers, including colleagues from Mexico who contributed a panel on the US/Mexico border. In its very difference, the region has striking parallels to the borderlands in which Ukraine and many countries on the edges of Europe find themselves today. *Both Sides Face East: Translation as Dialogue* will be our third volume.

Between No Limits / поміж без меж

It was not easy to find a name for our project and its location or *topos*. It seemed most meaningful to focus on Ukrainian writers in a way that reveals and establishes direct channels of communication between Ukraine and other minor (to use Deleuze's term) regions. The simplest way to indicate the scope of the project might have involved referring to Eastern Europe. This, however, would have limited us to the European continent, and also implicated us into a series of complex issues that we need to briefly acknowledge here.

"Eastern Europe" is not an easy term. In places such as Ukraine "both sides of the border face East," as Adam Zagajewski wrote in his poem "Granica" (Border). The dark shadow of Western Europe's colonial history until today obscures the regions that suffered not only from Western European, but also Russian imperialism. In the United States, for instance, few know about the complex history of the lands east of Berlin, west of Moscow, and north of Istanbul. Many are unaware not only of their internal differences, but also of the gorges and ravines of prejudice that separate them from their Western European neighbors. Soviet propaganda and other post-colonial discourses masked Russian colonialism, especially among the African, South Asian, and Latin American nations. As a result, the word "Europe" obscures and distorts the complex history and geography of the regions that suffered from both Western European and Russian colonial practices, and can stand in the way of forging alliances with other regions around the world.

The term "Eastern Europe" is problematic for yet another, diametrically opposed reason. If those outside the European continent are likely to have a negative reaction to the word "Europe," peoples from East Central and Eastern parts of this continent wish to distance themselves from the first word: "Eastern." Since the Age of Enlightenment the term "Eastern Europe" has a derogatory meaning. Western Europe constructed itself as more cultured and civilized by establishing a contrast with its margins. Most Eastern European nations wish to locate themselves—at the very least—in Central Europe. Until now, and especially in light of Russia's continued brutality, "Europe" for those on its geographical margins stands for the rule of law, freedom of speech, democratic institutions, safe neighborhoods. Embattled Ukrainians see "Europe" as a culmination of all that their Russian colonizer has been and is currently trying to take away from them, foremost their liberty and their lives. The word "Europe" condenses their ideals and aspirations at the same time as for many peoples outside of this continent it came to represent a heritage of violence, broken promises, unambiguous hypocrisy.

This is an example of what Miglena Nikolchina calls heterotopian homonymy. "Europe" means two radically different things: a left-leaning person from the United States hears "oppression," and a progressive Ukrainian—"liberation." This word blocks the possibility of understanding, it forecloses the space for discussion even before a conversation begins.

We opted for the title *Between No Limits / поміж без меж* that, like "Eastern Europe," is ambiguous by design, and avoids the double bind of "Europe."

Where We are Coming From

In the spirit of resisting double binds of all kinds, each editor wishes to place themself geographically, and in rough terms, position their experience of the project.

Julia Sushytska writes,

> Being oblivious to a truth—that you are hurting the person you love the most, or that your country launched a colonial war—is not a matter of intellectual abilities. The laws that govern our timespace and consciousness allow us to see—or not—something that might be staring us in the eye. The structure of in-between places—their topology—makes it more difficult to be blind to what is happening with me and around me. It affords fewer opportunities to protect and cultivate my blind spots.
>
> In-between places, including the region in which Ukraine is fighting for its freedom, are complex, ambiguous lands that have to confront not one, but several colonizing gazes. As a result, they contain more contradictions, making it difficult for their inhabitants to ignore and forget them. The tensions between identities and languages are more palpable—they irritate skin and leave marks on bodies. Coming from a mixed Polish-Ukrainian family, it is more difficult for me to become a Polish or a Ukrainian nationalist, and it is painful for me to see the blindness and the suffering of both. Without clear limits and borders, the in-between places are instances of Gloria Anzaldua's borderlands: those who traverse them cannot claim ethnic, racial, or linguistic purity. They are more likely to realize that they do not fully belong with any established identity. In-between timespaces also afford little opportunity for high moral ground—they are "flatter" than places that claim major status. It is easier for those who inhabit them to abandon claims to moral superiority.

Being ambiguous, borderlands make it difficult to exclude. It is the "major" powers that exclude themselves from the in-between and try to colonize it.

Living, or having lived for extended periods of time, in one of the in-between regions gives me a considerable advantage in taking up this epistemological position. Intimate knowledge of a borderland might even be a necessary—although not a sufficient—condition for developing a more complex understanding of myself and the world. Still, I must decide to locate myself in these lands tainted by ambivalence and paradox. I must give up the misleading safety of belonging to a nation, a language, a religion; of having an identity. I must abandon established narratives, signifiers, terminologies, theoretical frameworks, and points of reference.

An in-between place does not guarantee access to its epistemologically advantageous ground. I must make the effort of thinking, and continue making this effort—I cannot withhold the tensions of an in-between for long. Time and again I have to balance myself on the edges of languages and cultures, translate what resists translation, and respect the fragility of words while making them endure.

ariel rosé writes,

One of our participants asked, "But why this old concept of Eastern/Central Europe again?" Did this project risk being purely nostalgic? French philosopher Barbara Cassin asks a similar question in *Nostalgia: When Are We Ever at Home?*: "In what way . . . can we say that nostalgia is a feeling that defines Europe?" She answers by referring to Milan Kundera's definition in *The Art of the Novel*: "European: one who is nostalgic for Europe." With the annexation of Crimea by Russia and later with the escalation of the war in Ukraine in 2022, someone born in Ukraine or Poland will feel a difference from friends and colleagues from other places. Searching for a basis for this feeling—shared memory? Shared collective traumas? A particular sense of humor and irony? The border with Russia?—raises the question, do we make any "we" at all?

After the invasion of 2022, it was possible to document signs of solidarity with Ukraine throughout Europe: Ukrainian flags on apartment or shop windows, stickers and badges with Ukrainian flags, graffiti with encouraging words of support for Ukraine. Warsaw was full of them. Berlin lighted its Brandenburger Tor in yellow and blue. There was a moneybox to collect funds for Ukraine at the Paris Charles de Gaulle Airport, but the signs were less apparent the further south and west one traveled. In Arles, almost nobody wanted to talk about the war. The region had strong support for hard-right Marine Le Pen and hard-left Mélenchon, both with ties to Russia and its leadership. People in Italy used the word "conflict" instead of "war" for Russia's invasion of Ukraine. Iryna Shuvalova and Iya Kiva were invited for a book tour in Italy, but some universities were not interested in inviting them. Iryna shared with me her regret over blindness of the left in the West. Iryna and I define ourselves as leftists. Yet, some leftists in the West are nostalgic for Soviet communism and align with the Russian narrative, while we were oppressed by it. Readers were thoughtlessly asking Iryna uncomfortable questions after her reading, as if they knew her experience. She answered, "I am coming from Ukraine, would you like me to explain it to you?"

While at a writers' residency in Rome, I was invited for a poetry reading at La Sapienza University. Students gathered in the vast library of the Department of World Literature. The walls were empty, except for one. I stood opposite the wall. I read a poem for Iya Kiva, I talked about the war in Ukraine and felt a certain dissonance. In front of me—six portraits of melancholic men. Six Russian writers. No female writers. No other nationalities. In the Roman library. The portraits were from the seventies and were signed in Cyrillic.

Maybe the wall needed decolonization, refreshing? Lyuba Yakimchuk ended my conversation with her: "We understand, we know the Russians; they don't know us at all."

I come from a country, Poland, immersed in history. I grew up filled with narratives about history, especially World War II. There was a plaque, a monument, a sign reminding me of it on every corner. My generation felt grateful it was over, we believed it would not come back. Yet certain politicians would wake history up, like Putin. And it would wake up like a zombie. All the biggest fears materialized. Never before could I understand what Hannah Arendt meant by writing that sometimes history pushes us forward. With the escalation of the war in Ukraine, the history pushed me forward and for the first time in my life I live in the present.

At the same time, I see future in Ukraine. Ukraine speaks with various poetic voices. "I come from where . . . there is no language, only voices," writes Serhiy Zhadan. "The language in a time of war / can't be understood. Inside this sentence / is a hole—no one wants to die—no one / speaks," echoes Lesyk Panasiuk. "Teach me not to be silent," Marianna Kiyanovska adds to their chorus. Yet, they all speak up.

Borders in this part of Europe moved like vipers and people used to speak various languages. We can learn to use a language. Polish poet Czesław Miłosz wrote in *A Treatise on Poetry* that "a poet in Poland is a barometer"—a barometer cannot change the weather, and poets cannot change neither Poland, Ukraine nor the world. But, like a medicine that might not cure us, they relieve the pain or at least show us what's going on. A poem does not lie. It is honest.

Alisa Slaughter writes,

On a February evening in 2022, I was wrapping up a night class when one of my students looked up from her phone. "Russia just invaded Ukraine." Outside, it was hailing and the university had deployed lighted drones in the sky for a fundraising gala. Cold and dark, money and drones—it was a surreal pre-echo of what was to come.

The response to the invasion was similarly confusing, at least in the United States, a combination of heartening clarity and support, mixed messages; and jeering hostility. We embarked on this project with trepidation—what could literary people and philosophers contribute from positions of relative safety and with limited resources? The writers and translators who agreed to contribute to this volume helped me begin to understand the ambiguities and competing imperatives that prompted the project, directly or indirectly.

Outside a war zone or heat wave (and even there, when things are quiet for a few hours or a few days) the ants in the sugar bowl or a kid's meltdown over a school assignment may feel more urgent than big discourses and contradictory geopolitical imperatives. Nikolchina describes the mental effort to reconcile quotidian humanism and civic turmoil as "the fantasy of classical space," a place of equal access to intellectual conversation without interference from situated hierarchies or irrational pressures, in *Lost Unicorns of the Velvet Revolutions,* a book that has influenced our thinking about this one. The people Nikolchina describes struggled to reconcile their ideas; even coming up with a shared definition of "communist" or "totalitarian" Eastern Europe or theoretical frameworks like "Marxism" made people "switch off their hearing aids" rather than keep listening to what seemed like monstrous distortions of their ideals and experiences, their own fights with the ants and the homework—and the informant at work and the extortionate building supervisor, the inadequacies and outbursts of violence, the deprived and corrupt realities that confront all but the most privileged at some point.

Ukrainians and Gazans, Syrians and Sudanese and Haitians, all want the rabble out of their houses, they want their kids to go to school and turn in their homework, they want to be able to buy sugar without standing in lines or being flattened by bombs or tormented by gangsters. Outside the danger zones, alarm turns into anxiety: if only the war would end, if only the epidemic would run its course, if only this president or that party would win or lose an election, if only the people who assume any move toward social justice or effort to stave off climate disaster is *communist* or *woke* would lose their influence or withdraw from public life, everybody could get a breath, could look around and try to determine what will last, what is worth keeping, what needs to be changed, could claim our classical space like the lovable meliorists we are.

The constant barrage of atrocities from around the world insists that no one gets to take a breath—whatever began in 1989 (or 1933, or 1947, 1917, 1789, 1492, pick a date) moves, like Paul Klee's Angel of History, in only one direction without stopping. Being a meliorist automatically puts a person into the unlovable category. I may not be guilty (the wind blasts my face and blows me backward; I can't see the future, only the past) but I'm also, like most people, neither certain nor a sociopath, so I'm responsible, however painful the place in between feels. As Nikolchina describes her era, "some became convertible, the less convertible became depressive, the inconvertible died." Buffeted and breathless, struggling against the sadness and less than fully convertible, we offer these *durable words,* themselves contingent, incomplete, and of this moment.

Durable Words

Zsuzsa Selyem

We live in times of ephemeral words. A word that a second ago meant something now can have no meaning at all. The noise around us is too black. Innocent people are dying. Men and women with a lot of knowledge and capabilities to make the world a better place have gone to the armies to defend their homes and their beloved ones. We have seen the documentaries about their life on the front. It is indescribable, but we have to find the words for it, however painful they would be.

Meanwhile, aggressive political propaganda is flourishing worldwide. I come from Romania, but I belong to its Hungarian minority. My mother tongue is Hungarian, my basic cultural context is Hungarian, but not that Hungarian Viktor Orbán and his far-right opportunist gang speak about. Orbán, as one of Putin's lackeys, speaks and understands only oppressive, cynical language. Their language does not connect people and different traditions, their language is only a tool for preserving their power. Otherwise, they would have to face the court of justice for their criminal deeds. But no language is selfish, it would be a contradiction in itself. Dictators violate language for the sake of selfishness by suppressing critical voices, shutting down the media of the opposition, introducing censorship, controlling education. All literature is a scream across the sky against the reification of language by murderous powers.

There is a strong tradition in Hungarian literature that liberates by revealing how the language of oppressors functions (for instance, Géza Ottlik's *The School at the Frontier*, Imre Kertész's *Fatelessness*, or Péter Nádas's *Parallel Stories*):

- it has no words for suffering; moreover, it bans the words for suffering;
- it uses either euphemisms or curses, but even by chance it cannot be accurate;

- by means of metaphors it makes people get used to, familiarized to, oppression, discrimination, war;
- it is deeply exclusivist and it propagates exclusivism;
- it works with such emotions as fear, suspicion, distrust, hate;
- it objectifies.

But the words of the aggressive power are self-devouring as it hates even itself. Orbán's regime, for instance, is destroying the lives of its citizens: it ruins the educational system (while elites send their children to expensive private schools), the health system (when Orbán had health issues, he went to a private Austrian clinic), a massive part of the population lives in deep poverty without any means to improve their lives, people belonging to sexual or ethnic minorities are made the target of hate speech and are deprived by their civil rights, etc. The propaganda machine of the Hungarian government is ruining the very basis of democracy, mutual trust. The population has become so divided that even during a family dinner you have to agree to avoid politics.

During the good old days of socialist realism, mainstream literature and art was propaganda, the useful idiot of the dictatorship. Nowadays propaganda plays a sweeter tune to accompany the dance. A writer does not have to praise the power; it will do to keep quiet about its real face.

But how would you have words for connecting people if you respect these soft criteria of power? Literature does not use words, literature is in a creative, infinite, and personal relationship with them. Getting in touch with words is a risky activity, it cannot be described in terms of control.

Not long ago, the philosopher G. M. Tamás spoke about the overwhelming, global success of post-fascism in front of a resistant group of young people, and someone asked, is there some hope for us? He answered with a question (the most durable structure that can be made of words): who would have thought in the fourth century, when the Cappadocian Fathers condemned Plato's works, that a time will come when they are read worldwide?

Lviv, June 30, 2023

Довічні слова

Жужа Сельєм

Ми живемо у час ефемерних слів. Слово, яке ще мить тому мало значення, зараз може його втратити. Шум навколо нас надто вже чорний. Гинуть невинні люди. Чоловіки і жінки з усіма своїми знаннями і можливостями зробити світ кращим, змушені боронити свої домівки і близьких із зброєю в руках. Документальні фільми доносять до нас відгомін їхнього життя на фронті. Це неможливо описати, але хоч наскільки це боляче, ми мусимо знаходити для цього слова.

Тим часом, в усьому світі процвітає агресивна політична пропаганда. Я родом з Румунії, але належу до її угорської меншини, моя рідна мова — угорська, угорським є й мій основний культурний контекст. Але це не та угорська, якою розмовляє Віктор Орбан і його ультраправа опортуністична банда. Орбан, як і годиться путінській повії, знає лише деспотичну, цинічну мову. Ця мова не об'єднує людей і різні традиції, вона — лише інструмент для збереження влади. Інакше-бо люди на кшталт Орбана давно постали перед судом за свої злочини. Але ж мова за визначенням не може бути егоїстичною. Заради свого егоїзму, диктатори вивертають мову навиворіт, придушуючи критичні голоси, закриваючи ЗМІ опозиції, запроваджуючи цензуру, контролюючи освіту. Уся література — це всесвітній протест проти привласнення мови злочинною владою.

В угорській літературі проведена чітка лінія порятунку справжньої мови через розкриття особливостей мови гнобителів (наприклад, «Школа на кордоні» Ґези Оттліка, «Безжиттєвість» Імре Кертеша чи «Паралельні історії» Петера Надаша). Така мова

– не має слів на позначення страждання, ба більше — забороняє слова на позначення страждання,
– використовує евфемізми, або закляття, але навіть випадково не говорить точно,
– за допомогою метафор змушує людей призвичаюватись до гноблення, дискримінації, війни,
– є глибоко ексклюзивістською і пропагує ексклюзивізм,
– апелює до таких емоцій, як страх, підозра, недовіра, ненависть,
– об'єктивізує.

Але при цьому слова агресивної влади пожирають самих себе, адже її ненависть розповсюджується навіть на неї саму. Зокрема, режим Орбана підточує самі життєві можливості своїх громадян: система освіти ним повністю зруйнована (при цьому самі високопосадовці віддають своїх дітей до дорогих приватних шкіл), система охорони здоров'я також (коли в Орбана виникли проблеми зі здоров'ям, він звернувся до австрійської приватної клініки), величезна частина населення живе в глибокій бідності, не маючи жодних засобів для поліпшення свого життя, люди, що належать до сексуальних або етнічних меншин, стають мішенню для розпалювання ворожнечі і позбавлені своїх громадянських прав тощо. Пропагандистська машина угорського уряду руйнує саму основу демократії, довіру один до одного, тому населення настільки роз'єднане, що навіть під час сімейної вечері всі попередньо домовляються, що не говоритимуть про політику.

У старі добрі часи соцреалізму література та мистецтво звелися до пропаганди, цього корисного для диктатури ідіотизму. Сьогодні пропаганда танцює більш звабливо. Письменникові вже не обов'язково вихваляти владу, достатньо промовчати про її справжнє обличчя.

Та варто підпасти цьому м'якому тиску влади, як джерело слів для об'єднання людей миттєво пересихає. Література-бо не використовує слова, вона перебуває з ними в інтимних творчих стосунках. А такі стосунки зі словами засновані на ризику і несподіванці, жодного контролю вони не терплять.

Нещодавно філософ Гашпар Миклош Тамаш говорив про приголомшливий, глобальний успіх постфашизму перед групою молодих людей, і хтось запитав, чи для нас є якась надія. Він відповів питанням (найміцніша структура, яку можна звести зі слів): чи ж міг хто подумати у IV столітті, коли Каппадокійські отці засуджували Платона, що настануть часи, коли його твори читатимуть у всьому світі?

Львів, 30 травня 2023

Translated by Andriy Lysenko

Three Poems

Сергій Жадан

***

І тоді митник записав до книги моє ім'я.
— Чия це смужка землі, Господи?
— Нічия.
Відстань звідси додому — єдина величина.
Я шепочу вві сні:
Галичина, Галичина.
Я з тієї частини світу, де горять ліси,
де немає мови — є лише голоси,
де смерть щоранку перетинає кордон,
де з богом тебе поєднує шкільний коридор.
Там і до церкви йдуть, аби припасти до його щоки.
Там за мною досі плачуть заміжні жінки.
Там на села падає сніг зернами кришталю.
Там залишилось все, що я люблю.
Впиши мене до своєї книги, апостоле темноти.
Мою особу підтвердять морські кити.
Світиться білим камінням церква нічна.
Повторюй, апостоле, за мною:
Галичина, Галичина.
Стояти на цій землі, в своєму гурті.
Ще стільки потрібно встигнути в цьому житті:
навчити абетки довколишню дітвору,
полюбити землю, в якій помру.
Напиши про мене так: зимове взуття,

сіра сорочка,
довге життя,
темні очі, зубні коронки, шрам на щоці,
порядковий номер наколотий в таборі на кулаці.
А внизу допиши:
немає вини
в тій любові, яку несуть усі вони,
в тій печалі, яка за ними стоїть,
в пам'яті, яку вони проносять між століть.
Жодної вини,
жодного зла.
Жодного непотрібного ремесла.
Вписаний в книгу, будеш літерою в псалмі.
Діти виростуть, прочитають усе самі.

6 червня 2017

Тріска

1

Вона відчуває животом теплий потік
і прориває води посріблене волокно.
У вересні висушується материк,
під спресованою водою світиться дно.
У вересні атлантична тріска починає свій шлях,
рушає через потоки в бік зими.
Люди збирають збіжжя на осінніх полях.
Людям важливо завжди лишатись людьми.

2

Вона любить цей океан, що темніє свинцем,
любить небо над ним — щоранку нове.
Євразійський берег схожий на лице
людини, яка надто довго живе.
Починається осінь, закінчується рік.
Серпень лишає стільки шрамів і ран.
Цілу осінь через відкриті надрізи рік
тепло материка стікатиме в океан.

3

Ціле літо вона слухає голоси,
вислуховуючи з-поміж них той один,
який скаже їй: тепер уже час, неси,
неси свій тяж серед нічних глибин.
Неси його, ховай його у собі,
борони це нове життя в сріблі й свинці.
Кам'яний маяк стоїть на смарагдовому горбі.
Розкажеш потім, що там було, наприкінці.

4

І вона повертається у вересневій воді
і починає рух, що триватиме до весни.
Навесні вона, врешті, зупиниться, і тоді
нове життя підійметься з глибини.
Нове життя пробиватиме собі шлях,
повертатиметься до кам'яних заток.
Діти народжуються тоді, коли відступає страх,
коли не страшно зробити перший подих, перший ковток.

5

Голос їй сказав: не можна не бачити меж,
на всіх тисне важкий океанський прес,
але доки ти не зупиняєшся і пливеш,
у цьому всьому далі лишається сенс.
І його достатньо, аби тримати світ.
Все знову вирішиться навесні.
Білий, ніби покров богородиці, твій живіт
світить усім, хто лежить на дні.

6

Навесні все буде так, як уже було.
Приплив розбиває пагорби, мов таран.
І твоє тепло — зараз єдине тепло,
єдине тепло на увесь цей океан.
Вітер починає свої звичні плачі
і, ніби народи, підіймає жовті піски.
Хтось дбайливо прокладає вночі
підводні маршрути для молодої тріски.

7
Осіння земля дивиться їй услід.
Услід їй дивляться маяки.
І на гірських хребтах уже накипає лід,
і теплий дим підіймається від ріки.
Услід їй дивляться сосни з берегів,
дивляться собор та університет.
Там є книги про відступників та богів,
і небо складається з відкритих кимось планет.

8
Такий складний світ, — думає вона собі, —
у ньому стільки не потрібних нікому слів.
Місто прокидається на вітряному горбі,
сонце ховається між олив.
У вересні всі тіні такі замалі.
І поява холоду така різка.
Небо ранньої осені, небо землі —
послухай, як тебе славить вдячна тріска.

9
Вона відчуває животом дотик руки,
бачить світло в зеленій воді.
Шматками льоду обвалюються зірки.
Дерева, що ростуть на горбах, особливо тверді.
Коли допливеш, нагадай йому,
як нам бракує його мудрих казок.
Берег із вдячністю занурюється у пітьму.
Океан із радістю викидається на пісок.

10
І вона повертається і пірнає в потік,
і сонце з місяцем рухаються, як завжди,
і скільки має витекти рік,
щоби світові стало вологи, стало води.
І скільки має постійно битись сердець,

щоби світ не зупинявся серед ночей.
Скільки всього очікує насамкінець.
Скільки потрібних слів. Скільки важливих речей.

1 червня 2017

+++
Знайомі поховали сина минулої зими.
Ще й зима була такою — дощі, громи.
Поховали по-тихому — у всіх купа справ.
За кого він воював? — питаю. Не знаємо, — кажуть, — за кого він воював.
За когось воював, — кажуть, — а за кого — не розбереш.
Яка тепер різниця, — кажуть, — хіба це щось змінює, врешті-решт?
Сам би в нього і запитав, а так — лови не лови.
Хоча, він би й не відповів — ховали без голови.
На третьому році війни ремонтують мости.
Я стільки всього про тебе знаю — кому б розповісти?
Знаю, наприклад, як ти виспівував цей мотив.
Я знаю твою сестру. Я її навіть любив.
Знаю, чого ти боявся, і навіть знаю чому.
Знаю, кого ти зустрів тієї зими і що говорив йому.
Ночі тепер такі — з попелу та заграв.
Ти завжди грав за сусідню школу.
А ось за кого ти воював?
Щороку приходити сюди, рвати суху траву.
Скопувати щороку землю — важку, неживу.
Щороку бачити стільки спокою і стільки лих.
До останнього вірити, що ти не стріляв по своїх.
За дощовими хвилями зникають птахи.
Попросити б когось про твої гріхи. Але що я знаю про твої гріхи?
Попросити б когось, щоби скінчились нарешті дощі.
Птахам простіше — вони взагалі не чули про спасіння душі.

11 травня 2017

Three Poems

Serhiy Zhadan

***

Then, the customs man wrote my name in a book.
—Whose strip of land is this, Lord?
—Nobody's.
The distance from here to home is the only measure.
I whisper in a dream:
Galicia, Galicia.
I come from where the forests burn,
where there is no language, only voices.
where death crosses the border each morning,
where the school hallway leads to god.
They still betray with a kiss in the churches there.
Married women still cry for me there.
Snow falls, seeds of crystal, on the villages.
Everything remains, all that I love.
Inscribe me in your book, apostle of darkness.
Whales of the sea will say who I am.
At night the church shines, white stone.
Repeat after me, apostle:
Galicia, Galicia.
To stand on this earth among your own.
You must accomplish so much in this life:
teach the ABC to some neighborhood kids,
learn to love the soil in which I will die.
Write about me this way: winter shoes,
gray shirt,

full of years,
dark eyes, capped teeth, scarred cheek,
camp ID number tattooed on the fist.
And add below that:
there is no guilt
in that love all of them bear,
in the sorrow standing behind them,
in the memory they carry across centuries.
No guilt at all,
no bad thing.
Nothing degenerates.
In the book, in one psalm, you will be one letter.
Children grow up, read it all by themselves.

June 6, 2017

Cod

1

She feels the warm current with her stomach
and breaks the silver-plated fiber of water.
In September, the mainland dries up,
under water shines under pressure.
Atlantic cod migrates in September,
it sets out through the current to winter's edge.
People harvest grain in autumn fields.
It's important that people always remain people.

2

She loves this ocean growing dark as lead,
loves the sky over it—new every morning.
The coast of Eurasia looks like the face
of a human being who's lived too long.
Autumn begins, the year ends.
August left so many scars and wounds.
Through the open incisions of rivers
the continent's warmth flows to the ocean.

3

In summer she listens to the voices,
straining to hear among them the one
that will tell her: now is the time, endure,
bear your weight among the night's depths.
Bear it, hide it in yourself,
protect this new life in silver and lead.
A stone beacon stands on the emerald hill.
Say, later, what was there at the end.

4

And she turns in the September water
and begins the movement that lasts until spring.
In spring she'll stop, and then
new life will come from the depths.
New life will set its route,
will come back to the stone lagoon.
Children are born when fear retreats,
when no one fears the first breath, the first sip.

5

The voice told her: you can't miss the edge,
that heavy ocean presses us all,
but as long as you swim and don't stop,
all of this will keep making sense.
This is sufficient to sustain the world.
It will clear up in the spring.
Your stomach, white as the Virgin's mantle,
illuminates all who lie underwater.

6

In spring, everything will be as it has been.
Tide batters and breaks the hills.
And your warmth is now the only warmth,
the only warmth for the entire ocean.
The wind begins its usual lament
and stirs up yellow sands like nations and peoples.

By night, someone, with great care, sets
underwater routes for the young cod.

7
Autumn soil follows her with its gaze.
Lighthouses watch as she sets out.
On the mountain ridges frost already heaves,
and steam rises from the river.
Pines gaze after her from the shores,
a cathedral and a university observe.
There are books there about apostates and gods,
the sky consists of planets someone named.

8
Such a complicated world, she tells herself.
It has so many words nobody needs.
A city is waking on a windy hill,
The sun hides among the olive trees.
In September, the shadows are too short.
And cold's arrival is so sharp.
Sky of early autumn, sky of earth-
Listen how the grateful cod praises you.

9
She feels with her stomach the touch of a hand,
sees light in green water.
Stars collapse as chunks of ice.
Trees grow tough on crouching hills.
When you swim to your goal, remind him,
how much we miss his wise fables.
Grateful shore sinks into darkness.
Ocean leaps onto the sand for joy.

10
She turns and dives into the torrent,
sun and moon stir as always,
and how many rivers must drain,

so the world has enough moisture, enough water.
And how many hearts must beat constantly,
so the world won't stop in the small hours.
What waits at the end.
How many necessary words. How much that is important.

June 1, 2017

***

Some friends buried their son last winter.
What a winter it was, too—rain, thunder.
A quiet burial—everyone has tons to do.
Who did he fight for?—I ask. We don't know, they say, who he fought for.
He fought for somebody, they say, but hard to say who.
What difference does it make now, they say, what does that change in the end?
You should have asked him yourself, to be sure.
He wouldn't have answered anyway—we buried him without his head.
During the third year of war they're fixing the bridges.
I know so much about you—who could I tell?
I know, for instance, how you liked to sing this tune.
I know your sister. I even loved her.
I know what you were afraid of, and I even know why.
I know who you met that winter and what you told him.
Nowadays nights are made out of ashes, and glow.
You always played for the rival school.
But who did you fight for?
To come here every year, to pull dry grass.
To plow up this wide earth—heavy, lifeless.
To see so much peace every year, and so many troubles.
To believe until the end that you did not fire at your own.
Birds disappear behind the waves of rain.
How to ask for forgiveness. But what do I know about your sins?
How to ask that the rains finally stop.
It's easier for the birds—they never heard of the soul's salvation.

May 11, 2017

Translated by Julia Sushytska and Alisa Slaughter

Three Poems

Serhij Żadan

***

Potem celnik wpisał moje imię do księgi
— Czyj jest ten pas ziemi, Panie?
— Niczyj.
Jedyną miarą jest dystans stąd do domu.
Szepczę przez sen:
Galicja, Galicja.
Jestem z tej części świata, gdzie płoną lasy,
gdzie nie ma mowy — są tylko głosy,
gdzie każdego ranka śmierć przekracza granicę
gdzie szkolny korytarz łączy cię z bogiem
Chodzą tam do cerkwi, by zdradzić pocałunkiem w policzek.
Płaczą tam za mną zamężne kobiety.
Śnieg pada ziarnami kryształu na wioski.
Wszystko, co kocham, tam zostało.
Wpisz mnie do swojej księgi, apostole ciemności.
Wieloryby w głębinie morskiej potwierdzą moją tożsamość.
Cerkwia nocą świeci białym kamieniem.
Powtarzaj za mną, apostole:
Galicja, Galicja.
Stać na tej ziemi, pomiędzy swoimi.
Jest wiele jeszcze do zrobienia w tym życiu:
nauczyć alfabetu dzieci z okolicy,
pokochać ziemię, na której umrę.
Napisz tak o mnie: zimowe buty,

szara koszula,
długie lata życia,
ciemne oczy, korony na zębach, blizna na policzku.
A poniżej dodaj:
jest bez winy
w miłości, którą wszyscy niosą,
w smutku sunącym za nimi,
w pamięci, którą taszczą przez wieki.
Żadnej winy,
żadnej złej rzeczy.
Żadnego niepotrzebnego rzemiosła.
Wpisany w księgę, będziesz literą psalmu.
Dzieci dorosną i same wszystko przeczytają.

6 czerwca 2017

Dorsz

1

Wyczuwa brzuchem ciepły prąd
a posrebrzane włókno przebija się przez wodę.
Kontynent we wrześniu wysycha,
pod ciśnieniem wody świeci dno.
Atlantycki dorsz we wrześniu wyrusza w drogę,
w górę strumieni ku zimie.
Ludzie zbierają jesienią zboże z pól.
Ważne, by ludzie pozostali ludźmi.

2

Ryba uwielbia, gdy ocean ciemnieje ołowiem,
Uwielbia niebo nad sobą — co ranek inne.
Euroazjatycki brzeg przypomina twarz
człowieka, który za długo żyje.
Zaczyna się jesień, kończy się rok.
Sierpień pozostawia tyle blizn i ran.
Całą jesień przez otwarte nacięcia rzek
ciepło kontynentu wpływa do oceanu.

3

Całe lato słyszy ryba głosy,
stara się wsłuchać w jeden z nich,
który mówi: nastał czas, nieś,
nieś swoje brzemię przez głębinę nocy.
Dźwigaj, schowaj w sobie,
chroń to nowe życie w srebrze i w ołowiu.
Na szmaragdowym wzgórzu stoi latarnia z kamienia.
Opowiesz potem, co tam było na końcu.

4

I obraca się ryba we wrześniowej wodzie
i zaczyna się ruch, który potrwa do wiosny.
Wiosną w końcu się zatrzyma i wtedy
nowe życie wyłoni się z głębiny.
Nowe życie wytyczy sobie drogę,
powróci do kamiennych zatok.
Dzieci się rodzą, gdy ustępuje strach,
gdy niestraszny pierwszy oddech, pierwszy łyk.

5

Głos do ryby mówił: nie przegapisz brzegu,
ciężka masa oceanu naciska na każdego,
ale dopóki nie zatrzymujesz się i płyniesz,
to nadal ma to wszystko sens.
I to wystarczy, by przetrwał świat.
Wszystko się wyjaśni na wiosnę.
Twój brzuch biały jak welon Bogurodzicy
oświeca całe dno.

6

Wiosną wszystko będzie tak, jak było.
Przypływ uderza we wzgórza jak taran.
Twoje ciepło jest teraz jedynym ciepłem,
Jedynym ciepłem pośród całego oceanu.
Wiatr intonuje swój typowy lament
i niczym ludzi i narody — wzburza żółty piasek.

Nocą ktoś starannie brukuje
podwodne szlaki dla młodych dorszy.

7

Jesienna ziemia ogląda się za rybą.
Opiekują się nią latarnie morskie.
Na pasmach górskich warstwa lodu wrze
i wstaje ciepły dym od rzeki.
Sosny na brzegu oglądają się za nią,
przypatrują się jej katedry, uniwersytety.
Są tam książki o apostatach i bogach,
na niebie krążą odkryte przez kogoś planety.

8

Jaki skomplikowany świat, myśli sobie,
jest tyle w nim niepotrzebnych słów.
Miasto budzi się na smaganym wiatrem wzgórzu,
słońce chowa się pomiędzy oliwne drzewa.
We wrześniu cienie są takie małe.
Pierwsze zimno mocno przeszywa.
Niebo wczesnej jesieni, niebo ziemi
— posłuchaj, jak ciebie wielbi wdzięczny dorsz.

9

Czuje ryba dotyk dłoni brzuchem,
widzi światło w zielonej wodzie.
Gwiazdy spadają niczym grudki lodu.
Drzewa na wzgórzach wyjątkowo potężne.
Jak dopłyniesz, przypomnij mu,
jak nam brakuje jego mądrych bajek.
Wdzięczny brzeg zanurza się w ciemności.
Ocean radośnie rzuca się na piaszczysty brzeg.

10

A ryba zawraca i nurkuje wgłąb nurtu,
kręcą się jak zazwyczaj słońce z księżycem,
ile rzek musi wyschnąć,

co by światu starczyło wilgoci, starczyło wody.
Ile serc musi ciągle bić,
by świat nie ustał w środku nocy.
Ile rzeczy czeka na końcu.
Ile słów potrzeba. Ile

1 czerwca 2017

***

Znajomi pochowali syna zeszłej zimy.
Co to była za zima — deszcze, grzmoty.
To był cichy pogrzeb — każdy ma masę roboty.
Po czyjej stronie walczył? — Pytam. Nie wiemy — mówią — po której stronie walczył.
Walczył o kogoś, mówią, ale trudno powiedzieć o kogo.
Jaka to teraz różnica, mówią, czy to cokolwiek zmieni?
Trzeba było go pytać wtedy, a teraz kto to wie.
Zresztą, i tak by nic nie powiedział — pochowaliśmy go bez głowy.
Trzeci rok wojny remontują mosty.
Tak dobrze ciebie znam — komu mam wszystko opowiedzieć?
Wiem, na przykład, jak lubiłeś śpiewać pewną melodię.
Znałem twoją siostrę. Kochałem ją nawet.
Wiem, czego się bałeś i wiem nawet czemu.
Wiem, kogo spotkałeś tej zimy i co jemu powiedziałeś.
Noce teraz są takie — z popiołu i żaru.
Zawsze grałeś w drugiej szkole, w rywalizacji.
Ale o kogo walczyłeś?
Przyjeżdżajcie tu co roku, rwijcie suchą trawę.
Urabiajcie szeroką ziemię — ciężką, bez życia.
Co roku tyle spokoju, co katastrof.
Do końca wierzcie, że nie strzelaliście do swoich.
Ptaki znikają w falach deszczu.
Poproś kogoś, by wstawił się za twoje grzechy. Ale co ja wiem o twoich grzechach?
Poproś kogoś, by w końcu przestał padać deszcz.
Ptakom jest łatwiej — nic nie słyszały o zbawieniu duszy.

11 maja 2017

Translated by ariel rosé

Зберегти все

Андрій Лисенко

Тарас Шевченко вважав, що обожнюваний ним Гоголь пише російською, бо «своєї мови не знає».[1] З численних спогадів сучасників і літературознавчих розвідок нам відомо, що Микола Васильович рідну мову не просто знав, а почасти нею й думав. То яке «незнання мови» мав на увазі український поет? Відповідь на це дає перший біограф Гоголя – Пантелеймон Куліш. Він вважав щастям, що Гоголь писав свої твори російською, адже українською володів не достатньо, аби висловитись з повною свободою. «Він не міг володіти малоросійською мовою настільки довершено, аби не зупинятись на кожному кроці... за нестачею форм і барв»,[2] – підсумовує свої роздуми Куліш.

І Куліш, і Шевченко чудово розуміли, у чому полягає обов'язок художника – видати максимум можливого для себе, аби створити направду добрий твір. Тож якщо російськомовний український письменник «не достатньо володіє українською», аби досягнути в ній абсолютної свободи виразу, то його обов'язок як художника писати російською. Адже будучи українським митцем, він принесе Батьківщині більше користі, коли створить геніальну річ російською, ніж якщо не надто зграбно писатиме українською.

Будучи громадянами України, ми повинні знати українську. Не більше. Якою мовою нам думати і висловлювати свої думки на папері, зумовлюється не політикою, а долею. Так вже сталось, що значна частина українців російськомовна. Та й що?

---

1 Шевченко Т. [Передмова до нездійсненого видання «Кобзаря»] // Шевченко Т. Повне зібр. творів: У 12 т. Т. 5. Київ, 2003. – с. 208.

2 Куліш П. Вибрані твори. Київ, 1969. – с. 485.

Має значення тільки те, ЩО ти говориш. Якою мовою це сказано, питання другорядне. Насамперед у випадку художника, що працює зі словом.

Кремль проголошує: Росія там, де російська мова. Та й що? Разом із тим він проголошує і те, що Росія там, де колись була Російська Імперія, а потім – Радянський Союз. Чому з другим ми не погоджуємось, а перше сприймаємо як належне? Та російська вже давно не Росія так само, як англійська вже давно не Англія!

Російську використовували і продовжують використовувати в якості інструменту імперського впливу. Безперечно. Але чому ми маємо змиритись з тим, що користуватись цим інструментом можуть лише вони? Навспак! Слід використати цей інструмент на власну користь. Достоту так само, як захоплені у ворога російські танки чудово йдуть у бій вже під українськими знаменами.

Має рацію Ігор Померанцев, кажучи. що ЇМ «не слід віддавати ані частки» російської.[3] Та вже тому тільки, що право на мову мають тільки ті, хто її творить, творячи на ній: німець Фонвізін, данець Даль, українець Гоголь, нащадок африканців Пушкін і нащадок шотландців Лермонтов. Вони, а не путінська кліка, що у житті жодної книжки не прочитала, а говорить навіть не російською, а універсальною мовою канцеляризмів.

Якщо нам щось і загрожує, то не російська, а погана російська, не російська культура, а російське безкультур'я. Планомірна русифікація загарбаних імперією територій полягала аж ніяк не у насадженні високої російської культури, а в люмпенізації, насадженні канцеляризмів і матірщини. Й метою цієї «русифікації» було не зробити нас росіянами, а зробити нас ніким. Власне, саме ніким імперія спочатку зробила самих росіян – звідси зазначена багатьма авторами відсутність взаємопідтримки між етнічними росіянами у таборах, в'язницях, армії тощо.

Вчинимо ж навпаки! Проведемо дерусифікацію тим, що розвиватимемо культуру всіма мовами, якими говорить сучасна Україна: українською, російською, татарською, караїмською, польською, угорською тощо. На геніально написаний російською, татарською, польською чи угорською твір

---

3 Померанцев І., «Гуманітарний коридор».

знайдеться конгеніальний переклад на українську, а от на написані українською, але посередні твори жодного перекладача не знадобиться.

Відповідальність художника полягає у розумінні своїх можливостей і використанні своїх найсильніших сторін. Спробувати свої сили у новій мові – чому б ні? Але не ціною наступання собі на горлянку.

Львів, 2023

Keep It All

Andriy Lysenko

Taras Shevchenko believed that Mykola Gogol, whom he adored, wrote in Russian because he "does not know his own language."[4] From numerous recollections of contemporaries and literary studies, we know that Gogol not only knew Ukrainian, but also thought in it. So what kind of "ignorance of the language" did Shevchenko mean? Panteleimon Kulish, the first biographer of Gogol, answers this question. He considered it fortunate that Gogol wrote his works in Russian, because he did not know enough Ukrainian to express himself freely: He could not master Ukrainian "so perfectly as not to stop at every step... due to the lack of forms and colors."[5]

Both Kulish and Shevchenko perfectly understood what the artist's duty is - to give their utmost and create really good work. If a Russian-speaking Ukrainian writer "does not have sufficient mastery of Ukrainian" to achieve absolute freedom of expression in it, then it is their duty as an artist to write in Russian. A Ukrainian artist will be more useful by creating a work of genius in Russian than if they write clumsily in Ukrainian.

Citizens of Ukraine must know Ukrainian. Their public responsibility ends there. The private language we use to think and express our thoughts on paper

---

4 Taras Shevchenko, "Preface to an Unpublished Edition of *Kobzar*" in *Povne zibrannia tvoriv [Complete Works]*, vol. 5 (Kyiv: Naukova Dumka, 2003), 208. For the English translation see *Towards Intellectual History of Ukraine: An Anthology of Ukrainian Thought from 1710 to 1995*, ed. Ralph Lindheim and George S.N. Luckyj (Toronto: University of Toronto Press, 1996).

5 Panteleimon Kulish, "Epilogue to The Black Council: On the Relation of Little Russian Literature to Common-Russian Literature" in *Vybrani Tvory* [Selected Writings] (Kyiv, 1969), 485. English translation in *Towards Intellectual History of Ukraine.*

is determined not by politics, but by fate. Fate has determined that a significant number of Ukrainians now speak Russian. And so?

The only thing that matters is *what* you say. The question of language is secondary, especially for an artist who works with words.

The Kremlin proclaims: Russia is where the Russian language is. Simultaneously it declares that Russia is where the Russian Empire once was, and then the Soviet Union. Why do we disagree with the second, but take the first for granted? The Russian language has not belonged to Russia for a long time, just as English doesn't belong exclusively to England!

Russian was used and continues to be used as a tool of imperial influence. Of course. But why should we accept that only *they* can use this tool? On the contrary: we should use this tool to our advantage, in the same way that Russian tanks captured from the enemy win battles under Ukrainian flags.

Ihor Pomerantsev is right: we should not give them "even a small share" of Russian,[6] if only because only those who create it, by creating in it, have the right to it: Denis Fonvizin, a German, Vladimir Dal, a Dane, Mykola Gogol, a Ukrainian, Alexander Pushkin, a descendant of Africans, and Mikhail Lermontov, of Scottish descent. They have a right to the language, unlike Putin's clique, who have never read a single book in their life, and don't even speak Russian, but the universal wooden language of bureaucracy.

What threatens us speaks not in Russian, but in bad Russian; it is not Russian culture, but Russian lack of culture. The systemic Russification of the territories conquered by the empire planted a lumpen bureaucracy and disgusting language, not a refined Russian culture. The goal of this "Russification" was not to make us Russians, but to make us nobody. In fact, the empire first made the Russians themselves nobody - hence the lack of mutual support in camps, prisons, and the army, noted by many Russian writers.

Let's do the opposite, let's carry out de-Russification by developing culture in all the languages spoken in Ukraine: Ukrainian, Russian, Tatar, Karaite, Polish, Hungarian. A Ukrainian translation will reflect a brilliant original in Russian, Tatar, Polish or Hungarian, but works written in mediocre Ukrainian will not benefit from any translator.

---

6 Igor Pomerantsev, "Humanitarian Corridor" (included in this volume).

The artist's responsibility lies in understanding their capabilities and strengths. Nothing stops a writer from trying out a new language, but they should be careful not to put their knee on their own throat.

Lviv, 2023

Translated by Alisa Slaughter and Julia Sushytska

ZADRŽI SVE

Andriy Lysenko

Taras Shevchenko je smatrao da Gogolj, kojeg je obožavao, piše na ruskom jer „ne poznaje svoj jezik." Iz brojnih sjećanja njegovih suvremenika i književnih studija znamo da je Gogolj ne samo poznavao ukrajinski, nego je na njemu i mislio. Na kakvo je, dakle, „nepoznavanje jezika" Shevchenko mislio?

Panteleimon Kulish, prvi Gogoljev biograf, ima odgovor na to. Smatrao je srećom što je Gogolj svoja djela pisao na ruskom, jer ukrajinski jezik nije dovoljno znao da bi se potpuno slobodno izražavao: „Nije mogao svladati ukrajinski jezik tako savršeno da ne zastaje na svakom koraku... zbog nedostatka oblika i boja."

I Kulish i Shevchenko savršeno razumiju šta je dužnost umjetnika—to jest, dati sve od sebe kako bi mogli stvoriti dobro djelo. Dakle, ako ukrajinski pisac koji govori ruski „ne poznaje dovoljno dobro ukrajinski" da postigne apsolutnu slobodu izražavanja na njemu, onda je njegova dužnost kao umjetnik pisati na ruskom. Ukrajinski će umjetnik biti neophodniji ako stvori briljantno djelo na ruskom nego ako nespretno piše na ukrajinskom.

Budući da smo građani Ukrajine, moramo znati ukrajinski. Naša javna odgovornost tu i počinje i prestaje. A to na kojem ćemo jeziku misliti i izražavati svoje misli na papiru ne određuje politika, već sudbina. Sudbina je već odredila da značajan broj Ukrajinaca sada govori ruski. I šta sad?

Važno je samo šta se govori. Na kojem jeziku je to rečeno—to je sporedno pitanje, pogotovo za umjetnika koji radi s riječima. Kremlj poručuje: Rusija je tamo gdje je ruski jezik. I šta sad? Istovremeno izjavljuje da je Rusija tamo gdje je nekad bilo Rusko Carstvo, a zatim Sovjetski Savez. Zašto se ne slažemo s drugim, a prvo uzimamo zdravo za gotovo? Ruski jezik odavno ne pripada Rusiji, kao što ni engleski ne pripada isključivo Engleskoj!

Ruski se koristio i nastavlja se koristiti kao sredstvo imperijalnog utjecaja. Naravno. Ali zašto bismo mi to prihvatili, da samo *oni tamo* mogu koristiti taj instrument? Baš naprotiv: trebali bismo koristiti taj instrument u svoju korist, na isti način na koji ruski tenkovi uhvaćeni od neprijatelja idu u bitku pod ukrajinskim zastavama.

Ihor Pomerantsev je u pravu: da njima ne treba dati „čak ni djelić" ruskog, pa makar zato što samo oni koji ga stvaraju, stvarajući u njemu, imaju pravo na njega: Nijemac Denis Fonvizin, Danac Vladimir Dal, Ukrajinac Gogolj, potomci Afrikanaca Puškin i Ljermontov. Oni ne pripadaju Putinovoj ekipi koja ni jednu knjigu u životu nije pročitala, pa čak ni ne govori na ruskom, već univerzalni odrvenjeni jezik birokracije.

Ono što nam prijeti ne govori samo ruski, nego loš ruski, nije ruska kultura, nego ruska nekultura. Sustavna rusifikacija teritorija koje je carstvo osvojilo nije usadilo profinjenu rusku kulturu, nego lumpenizaciju, atrofiranu birokraciju i nakaradan jezik.

A cilj te „rusifikacije" nije bio da postanemo Rusi, nego da postanemo niko. Zapravo, carstvo je najprije svoje Ruse činilo nikim—otuda je i krenuo njihov nedostatak međusobne podrške u logorima, zatvorima, vojsci, itd., kako su mnogi ruski pisci odavno primijetili. Da učinimo suprotno! Izvršimo derusifikaciju razvijajući kulturu na svim jezicima koji se govore u današnjoj Ukrajini: na ukrajinskom, ruskom, tatarskom, karaitskom, poljskom, mađarskom, itd. Djelo briljantno napisano na ruskom, tatarskom, poljskom—na bilo kojem jeziku—će biti prevedeno na ukrajinski na prikladan način, a djelo napisano na osrednjem ukrajinskom neće trebati niti imati korist od bilo kojeg prevodioca.

Odgovornost umjetnika je razumjeti svoje sposobnosti i iskoristiti svoje snage. Ništa ne sprječava pisca da isproba novi jezik, ali treba paziti da ne stane sebi na grlo.

Lviv, 2023

Translated by Ena Selimović

Gardons Tout !

Andreï Lysenko

Taras Chevtchenko croyait que Nicolas Gogol, qu'il adorait, écrivait en russe parce qu'il "ne connaissait pas sa propre langue"[7]. D'après de nombreux témoignages contemporains et essais littéraires, nous savons que Gogol non seulement connaissait l'ukrainien, mais pensait aussi en ukrainien. Alors, de quel genre d' "ignorance de la langue" Chevtchenko voulait-il parler ? Panteleimon Kulish, le premier biographe de Gogol, a répondu à cette question. Il considérait comme une chance que Gogol ait écrit ses œuvres en russe, car il ne connaissait pas suffisamment l'ukrainien pour s'exprimer spontanément dans cette langue : il ne le maîtrisait pas « suffisamment bien pour ne pas s'arrêter à chaque pas... faute de trouver les formes et les couleurs »[8].

Kulish et Chevtchenko ont parfaitement compris le devoir de l'artiste - donner le maximum et créer un très bon travail. Si un écrivain ukrainien russophone "n'a pas une maîtrise suffisante de l'ukrainien" pour y parvenir avec toute la liberté d'expression voulue, alors il est de son devoir d'artiste d'écrire en russe. Un artiste ukrainien sera plus utile en créant une œuvre de génie en russe que s'il écrit maladroitement en ukrainien.

Les citoyens ukrainiens doivent connaître l'ukrainien. Leur responsabilité publique s'arrête là. Le langage privé que nous utilisons pour penser et exprimer nos pensées sur le papier n'est pas déterminé par la politique, mais par le destin. Le destin a déterminé qu'un nombre important d'Ukrainiens parlent maintenant le russe. Et alors ?

---

7 Chevtchenko T. [avant-propos inédit pour une édition de « Kobzar »].

8 Koulich P. «*Sur les rapports de la littérature de la Petite Russie avec la littérature russe dans son ensemble*».

La seule chose qui compte, c'est ce que vous dites. La question de la langue est secondaire, surtout pour un artiste qui travaille avec les mots.

Le Kremlin proclame : la Russie est là où est la langue russe. Simultanément, il déclare que la Russie est là où se trouvait autrefois l'Empire russe, puis l'Union soviétique. Pourquoi sommes-nous en désaccord avec la deuxième proposition mais tenons-nous la première pour acquise ? La langue russe n'appartient plus à la Russie depuis longtemps, tout comme l'anglais n'appartient plus exclusivement à l'Angleterre !

Le russe a été utilisé et continue d'être utilisé comme un outil de l'influence impériale. Bien sûr. Mais pourquoi devrions-nous accepter qu'eux seuls puissent l'utiliser ? Au contraire : nous devrions détourner cet outil à notre avantage, à la manière dont nous utilisons les chars russes capturés à l'ennemi pour gagner des batailles sous drapeaux ukrainiens.

Igor Pomerantsev a raison : il ne faut pas leur laisser « même une petite part » de russe[9], entre autre parce que seuls ceux qui créent la langue, en créant en son sein, en ont le droit : Denis Fonvizine, un Allemand, Vladimir Dal, un Danois, Nicolas Gogol, un Ukrainien, Alexandre Pouchkine, un descendant d'Africains, et Mikhail Lermontov, d'origine écossaise. Ils ont droit à cette langue, contrairement à Poutine et à sa clique, qui n'ont jamais lu un seul livre de leur vie, et qui ne parlent même pas le russe, mais la langue de bois universelle de la bureaucratie.

Ce qui nous menace ne parle pas russe, mais un mauvais russe, ce n'est pas la culture russe, mais l'absence de culture russe. La russification systémique des territoires conquis par l'empire a enraciné une sous-bureaucratie et un langage écoeurant, pas une culture russe raffinée. Le but de cette « russification » n'était pas de faire de nous des Russes, mais de nous annihiler. En fait, l'empire a d'abord annihilé les russes - d'où le manque de solidarité dans les camps, les prisons et l'armée, relevé par de nombreux écrivains russes.

Faisons le contraire, procédons à une dé-russification en développant la culture dans toutes les langues parlées en Ukraine : ukrainien, russe, tatar, karaïte, polonais, hongrois. Une traduction en ukrainien reflétera toujours un original brillant en russe, tatar, polonais ou hongrois, mais les œuvres écrites dans un ukrainien médiocre ne trouveront aucun traducteur.

---

9 Pomerantsev I. "Humanitarian Corridor" (inclu dans ce volume).

La responsabilité de l'artiste réside dans la compréhension de ses capacités et de ses forces. Rien n'empêche un écrivain de s'essayer à une nouvelle langue, mais il doit faire attention à ne pas se mettre un couteau sous la gorge.

Lviv, 2023

Translated by Céline Anger

Zachować wszystko

Andrzej Łysenko

Taras Szewczenko uważał, że Mykoła Gogol, którego uwielbiał, pisał po rosyjsku, ponieważ „nie znał swojego języka".[10] Z licznych wspomnień i badań literackich wiemy, że Gogol nie tylko znał ukraiński, ale także myślał w tym języku. Jaką zatem „nieznajomość języka" miał na myśli Szewczenko? Odpowiedzi udziela pierwszy biograf Gogola, Pantelejmon Kulisz. Uważał, że dobrze się stało, że Gogol pisał swoje dzieła po rosyjsku, ponieważ nie znał ukraińskiego na tyle, aby się w tym języku swobodnie wypowiadać: "Nie potrafił opanować małorosyjskiego na tyle doskonale, aby nie zatrzymywać się na każdym kroku... z powodu braku form i kolorów".[11]

Zarówno Kulisz, jak i Szewczenko doskonale rozumieli, na czym polega obowiązek artysty – dać z siebie wszystko, aby stworzyć prawdziwie wartościowe dzieło. Jeśli więc rosyjskojęzyczny pisarz ukraiński „nie zna języka ukraińskiego na tyle", aby osiągnąć w nim absolutną swobodę wypowiedzi, to jego obowiązkiem jako artysty jest pisanie po rosyjsku. Będąc ukraińskim artystą, więcej pożytku przyniesie ojczyźnie, gdy stworzy coś genialnego po rosyjsku, niż gdyby pisał niezdarnie po ukraińsku.

Obywatele Ukrainy muszą znać język ukraiński. Ich publiczna odpowiedzialność kończy się na tym. Prywatny język, którego używamy do myślenia i wyrażania myśli na papierze, jest determinowany nie przez politykę, ale przez los. Los sprawił, że znaczna liczba Ukraińców mówi teraz po rosyjsku. I co z tym zrobić?

---

10 Taras Szewczenko, „Przedmowa do nieopublikowanego wydania *Kobzara*."
11 Pantełejmon Kulisz, „Epilog do *Czarnej rady*: o stosunku literatury małorosyjskiej do literatury ogólnorosyjskiej."

Liczy się jedynie to, co się mówi. Kwestia języka jest drugorzędna, zwłaszcza w przypadku artysty pracującego słowem.

Kreml głosi: Rosja jest tam, gdzie jest język rosyjski. Jednocześnie oświadcza, że Rosja jest tam, gdzie kiedyś było Imperium Rosyjskie, a potem Związek Radziecki. Dlaczego nie zgadzamy się z drugim, ale przyjmujemy pierwsze za pewnik? Język rosyjski od dawna nie należy do Rosji, tak jak angielski nie należy wyłącznie do Anglii!

Język rosyjski był i jest nadal używany jako narzędzie imperialnego wpływu. Zdecydowanie. Ale dlaczego mielibyśmy zaakceptować, że tylko obywatele Rosji mogą używać tego narzędzia? Wręcz przeciwnie: powinniśmy używać tego samego narzędzia na naszą korzyść. Rosyjskie czołgi odebrane wrogowi idą do boju pod ukraińskimi banderami.

Ihor Pomerantsev ma rację: nie powinniśmy dawać im "nawet ułamka" języka rosyjskiego.[12] Choćby dlatego, że prawo do języka mają tylko ci, którzy go tworzą, tworząc w nim: Niemiec Denis Fonwizin, Duńczyk Władimir Dal, Ukrainiec Mykoła Gogol, potomek Afrykanów Aleksander Puszkin i potomek Szkotów Michaił Lermontow. Mają prawo do języka, w przeciwieństwie do kliki Putina, która nigdy w życiu nie przeczytała ani jednej książki i nawet nie mówi po rosyjsku, ale uniwersalnym drewnianym językiem biurokracji.

Jeśli coś nam zagraża, to nie Rosja, ale zła Rosja, nie rosyjska kultura, ale rosyjski brak kultury. Systemowa rusyfikacja ziem podbitych przez imperium zasiała lumpenbiurokrację i okropny język, a nie wyrafinowaną rosyjską kulturę. Celem zaś tej „rusyfikacji" nie było uczynienie z nas Rosjan, ale uczynienie z nas nikogo, mieliśmy stać się nikim. Właściwie to imperium początkowo uczyniło samych Rosjan nikim – stąd brak wzajemnego wsparcia pomiędzy etnicznymi Rosjanami w obozach, więzieniach, wojsku, który został odnotowany przez wielu rosyjskich autorów.

Zróbmy odwrotnie, przeprowadźmy derusyfikację poprzez rozwój kultury we wszystkich językach, którymi mówi współczesna Ukraina: ukraińskim, rosyjskim, tatarskim, karaimskim, polskim, węgierskim itd. Ukraińskie tłumaczenie będzie odzwierciedlać genialny oryginał w języku rosyjskim, tatarskim,

---

12 Igor Pomerantsev, „Korytarz humanitarny" (w tym tomie).

polskim lub węgierskim, natomiast do dzieł napisanych po ukraińsku, ale przeciętnie, nie będzie potrzebny tłumacz.

Odpowiedzialność artysty polega na zrozumieniu swoich możliwości i mocnych stron. Nic nie powstrzymuje pisarza przed wypróbowaniem nowego języka, ale powinien uważać, by nie zamknąć sobie ust.

Lwów 2023

Translated by ariel rosé

Őrizd meg mind

Andrij Liszenko

Tarasz Sevcsenko azt hitte, hogy Mikola Gogol, akit egyébként imádott, azért írt oroszul, mert „nem ismeri az anyanyelvét".[13] Több korabeli megemlékezésből és irodalmi tanulmányból tudható, hogy Gogol nemcsak ismerte az ukrán nyelvet, de ukránul is gondolkodott. Akkor hát miféle nyelvi ignoranciára gondolhatott Sevcsenko? Panteleimon Kulis, Gogol első életrajzírója megválaszolja a kérdést. Szerencsének tartja, hogy Gogol oroszul írt, mert annyira jól azért csak nem tudott ukránul, hogy szabadon bánjon a nyelvvel: „nem ismerte olyan szinten, hogy ne kelljen megállnia minden lépésnél... a nyelvi formáknak és színeknek nem volt birtokában."[14]

Kulis és Sevcsenko pontosan tudták, mi egy művész dolga – hogy képességeiből a legtöbbet hozza ki, és igazán jó munkát végezzen. Ha egy oroszul beszélő ukrán író nem mestere az ukrán nyelvnek eléggé ahhoz, hogy abszolút szabadon fejezze ki magát, akkor az a dolga, hogy oroszul írjon. Az az ukrán művész, amelyik zseniális művet hoz létre oroszul, sokkal inkább segíti az ukrán kultúrát, mint az, aki ugyan ukránul ír, de ügyetlenül.

Ukrajna állampolgárai kell tudjanak ukránul. Civil kötelességei közé tartozik, de ennyi. Azt, hogy személyesen milyen nyelven gondolkodik, milyen nyelven ír, nem a politika határozza meg, hanem a sors. A sors hozta úgy, hogy az ukránok egy jelentős része oroszul beszél. És akkor mi van?

Az egyetlen dolog ami igazán számít, hogy *mit* mondasz. Hogy milyen nyelven, másodlagos, főként egy szavakkal dolgozó művész számára.

---

13 Tarasz Sevcsenko, „Előszó a *Kobzar* kéziratához in: *Povne zibrannia tvoriv* [*Complete Works*], vol. 5 (Kyiv: Naukova Dumka, 2003), 208. Angol fordításban lásd *Towards Intellectual History of Ukraine: An Anthology of Ukrainian thought from 1710 to 1995*, szerk. Ralph Lindheim és George S.N. Luckyj (Toronto: University of Toronto Press, 1996).

14 Panteleimon Kulis, „Utószó a Fekete Tanácshoz: A kis orosz irodalom és a közös orosz irodalom viszonyáról" in *Vybrani Tvory* [Válogatott írások] (Kyiv: 1969), 485. Angol fordításban: *Towards Intellectual History of Ukraine.*

A Kreml odanyilatkozott, hogy Oroszország ott van, ahol oroszul beszélnek. Ezzel párhuzamosan azt is kijelentette, hogy Oroszország ott van, ahol valaha az Orosz Birodalom és a Szovjetunió volt. Miért nem értünk egyet az utóbbival, és fogadjuk el az első kijelentést? Hosszú időn át az orosz nyelvet nem csupán Oroszországban beszélték, úgy ahogyan az angolt sem csak Angliában.

Az orosz nyelvet régen is, most is a birodalmi terjeszkedés érdekében használták. Persze. De miért kellene elfogadni azt, hogy csak *ők* használhatják? Éppen ellenkezőleg: nyugodtan kellene használnunk a saját érdekünkben, éppúgy, ahogyan az ellenségtől zsákmányolt orosz tankokkal csatákat nyerhetünk az ukrán zászló alatt.

Ihor Pomerancsevnek igaza van: nem kéne az orosz nyelv „még egy kis részét" sem átadnunk nekik,[15] mivel a nyelvhez mindazoknak joga van, akik megalkotják, művelik, műalkotásokat hoznak létre vele: a német Denis Fonvisin, a dán Vladimir Dal, az ukrán Mikola Gogol, a részben afrikai származású Alekszandr Puskin, vagy a skót származású Mihail Lermontov. Joguk van a nyelvhez, szemben Putyin klikkjével, akik egész életükben egy könyvet el nem olvastak, akik valójában nem is oroszul beszélnek, hanem a bürokrácia egyetemes fanyelvén.

Ami bennünket fenyeget, az nem oroszul beszél, hanem gyatra oroszul, a támadók nem az orosz kultúrát képviselik, hanem az orosz kultúra hiányát. A birodalom által elfoglalt területek szisztematikus oroszosítása egy lumpen bürokráciát és egy visszataszító nyelvet honosított meg, nem egy kifinomult orosz kultúrát. Az oroszosítás célja nem az volt, hogy oroszok legyünk, hanem az, hogy senkik legyünk. Valójában a birodalom előbb magukat az oroszokat tette senkikké – ezért van az, amiről beszámol több orosz író is, hogy nem segítenek egymásnak a harcmezőkön, a börtönökben, a hadseregben.

Tegyük ennek az ellenkezőjét, álljunk ellen úgy az erőszakos oroszosításnak, hogy az Ukrajnában beszélt nyelveken kultúrát hozunk létre: ukránul, oroszul, tatárul, karaimul, lengyelül, magyarul. A briliáns orosz, tatár, lengyel vagy magyar eredeti ukrán fordításban is ragyogni fog, de egy olyan ukrán szöveg, amely nem képes a nyelvet csak középszerűen használni, nem fog sokat hozzáadni kultúránkhoz.

A művész dolga tisztában lenni saját képességeivel és erősségeivel. Semmi nem állíthatja meg az írót abban, hogy egy új nyelvet próbáljon ki, de vigyáznia kell, hogy hangját kényszer ne fojtogassa.

Translated by Zsuzsa Selyem

---

15 Ihor Pomerancsev, "Humanitárius folyosó" (Humanitarian Corridor címmel megtalálható ebben a kötetben).

Леко Писане

Миглена Николчина

Това е историята на двама влюбени
разделени от един разказ
или по-точно от конфликта между фабула и сюжет
в един разказ
но и това не е съвсем точно, защото конфликтът
всъщност е
между фабула и фабула
между сюжет и сюжет
между между и между
Това е история с множество пистолети, но всички те
изгърмяват в други текстове
Прави каквото искаш с мене казва някой
дали тя? дали той?

Започваме отначало.
„Леко дишане“ е разказ на Бунин.
„„Леко дишане“ “ е есе на Виготски за разказа на Бунин.
„„„Леко дишане“ “ “ е епистоларно стихотворение
за двама влюбени
които четат „Леко дишане“
„„Леко дишане“ “
„„Леко дишане“ “ “

„„„„„„„„„„„„
“ “ “ “ “ “ “ “ “

Първо писмо. Тя до него:
Тя диша леко, той я застрелва.

Второ писмо. Той до нея:
Гнусният старец я целува през кърпичката,
тя се смее. Той я застрелва.

Трето писмо:
Старецът не е толкова стар, не е толкова гнусен,
тя го целува през кърпичката сякаш е някой друг
сякаш няма брада.
Тя владее тайната на лекотата.

Четвърто писмо:
Тя му показва дневника си с гнусния старец,
той я застрелва.
Тайната на лекотата е стрелбата,
лекият изстрел.

Пето писмо:
Тя пише, той я застрелва.

Бунин пише. Бунин пише!

Пише и я застрелва
Чете и я застрелва

Но що е фабула? що е сюжет?
сюжетът диша леко фабулата мре
Лекото дишане е изкуството на разказвача
Я ме чуй как поемам въздух!

Мъжът и въздухът — няма такова „и"
тя диша мъжете както си вкарва въздуха
не те не се дишат както се поема въздух
те имат бради понякога, понякога пистолети

тя трябва да се върне там където се диша
където любовта се диша

И все пак прави с мене каквото искаш
Прави с мене каквото искаш
Защото искам да правиш
Защото искам да искаш
Такъв е сюжетът фабулата
Ако има пистолет в началото на един разказ
Прави ме Убий ме Умри ме
Или я по-добре ми върни писмата

Семейотике

В последното стихотворение от този цикъл —
ако успеем аз и ти до там да стигнем —
ще прекосим в един дъждовен ден Autoroute du soleil.
Това ще се случва през деветдесетте, в края на века,
когато комунизмът трябваше вече да е обзел
по-добрата част от човечеството,
прекрасните мъже и особено жени на Иван Ефремов
трябваше да са слезли от мъглявината Андромеда
и да пристъпват по земя укротена като дрогиран
тигър,
под небеса пламтящи в трасета към квадрилионите
и квинтилионите.

Андромеда ще се появява в това възможно
стихотворение под формата на хотел,
със звездна карта във фоайето.
Ще бъде сумрачно по автострадата на слънцето
под изобилните оранжеви лампи на Белгия
и мъжът, който кара колата ще казва на някакъв
език любов моя

и ще пъха ръката си между краката на жената без
да я пита
и жената до него ще отговаря любов моя, но ще
мисли на своя си език

курво, мръснице, шенгенска путко.

Тя също ще го пипа където си иска
и той също ще си мисли каквото си иска.
Прочее желанието й към него не ще притури нищо
към онова, което си мисли за мъжете.
Всъщност те и двамата ще бъдат жени
или и двете ще бъдат мъже, побеснели швестерки,
тя ще бъде неговия butch, той ще бъде нейната femme,
gender trouble: she likes her girls to be boys,
телата им постоянно ще катапултират в
противоположното,
без никой вече да знае какво е противоположното,
стриктно осъдено,
поради което с тези функции ще се нагърбят
посоките на света.

Край на века, fin de siècle, the end с една дума, край,

край,

докато на английски идваме, на български
свършваме,
в мигове на екстаз той ще казва
hurt me, kill me

в мигове на екстаз тя ще казва
най-хубавото е че не ме разбираш
най хубавото е че влюбените не се докосват дори в
раните и в синините си

най хубавото е че поезията не прекосява никакви
граници дори своите собствени

най хубавото е че никой вече не я чете
най хубавото е че без точки и главни букви тя отнася
спираловидната си галактика по далечните ръбове на
невъзможното
и ни оставя по нашите автостради по нашите
граници

някои да ги пресичат други да висят по тях трети
да пропълзяват
под тях под оранжевите лампи под камионите
под самата Европейска общност. Ето кое е
най-хубавото my love amore mio
auf der autoroute du soleil.

Ще отбият от autoroute-а на слънцето по здрач, по
неосветен път,
съвсем тесен под оголените дървета, вкоренени във
времена отпреди автострадите.
Един изсъхнал лист ще прелети пред фаровете —
сгърчен, уголемен от сенките.
Жаба — ще каже той. Крастава жаба!
Използвали са я за лекове за потентност.

После ще види, че е сух лист, каква ти жаба през декември.
Ще види също, че тя е видяла, тя ще види, че той е
видял, видял е, че тя е видяла, че той е видял.

Ще продължат в мълчание.

Leichtes Schreiben

Miglena Nikoltschina

Das ist die Geschichte von zwei Verliebten
die eine Erzählung trennt
oder genauer von dem Konflikt zwischen Fabel und Sujet in einer Erzählung
aber auch das ist nicht ganz genau, weil der Konflikt in Wirklichkeit bestehi
zwischen Fabel und Fabel
zwischen Sujet und Sujet
zwischen zwischen und zwischen
Das ist eine Geschichte mit vielen Pistolen, aber sie gehen alle in anderen Texten los.
Mach mit mir was du willst sagt jemand vielleicht sie? vielleicht er?
Wir beginnen von vorn.
„Leichtes Atmen“ ist eine Erzählung von Bunin.
„„Leichtes Atmen““ ist ein Essay von Wigotskij über die Erzählung von Bu
„„„Leichtes Atmen“““ ist ein epistolares Gedicht über zwei Verliebte
die lesen „Leichtes Atmen“
„„Leichtes Atmen““
„„„Leichtes Atmen“““

Erster Brief. Sie an ihn:
Sie atmet leicht, er erschießt sie.

Zweiter Brief. Er an sie:
Der ekelige Alte küßt sie durch das Seidentüchlein,
sie lacht. Er erschießt sie.

Dritter Brief:
Der Alte ist nicht so alt, ist nicht so ekelig,
sie küßt ihn durch das Seidentüchlein, als wäre er jemand anderes,
als hätte er keinen Bart.
Sie beherrscht das Geheimnis der Leichtigkeit.

Vierter Brief:
Sie zeigt ihm ihr Tagebuch mit dem ekeligen Alten,
er erschießt sie.
Das Geheimnis der Leichtigkeit ist das Schießen,
der leichte Schuß.

Fünfter Brief:
Sie schreibt, er erschießt sie.

Bunin schreibt. Bunin schreibt!

Er schreibt und erschießt sie
Er liest und erschießt sie

Aber was ist Fabel? was ist Sujet?
das Sujet atmet leicht die Fabel stirbt
Das leichte Atmen ist die Kunst des Erzählers

Hör doch wie ich Luft hole!

Die Klassenlehrerin mag die Luft die sie
geatmet hat Aprilwind

Der Mann und die Luft — ein solches „und" gibt es nicht
sie atmet die Männer wie sie sich die Luft einverleibt
nein sie lassen sich nicht atmen wie man Luft holt
manchmal haben sie Barte, manchmal Pistolen
sie muß ausbreiten — aber was?
dorthin zurückgehen wo geatmet wird
wo die Liebe geatmet wird

Und trotzdem mach mit mir was du willst

Mach mit mir was du willst
Weil ich will daß du machst
Weil ich will daß du willst
So ist das Sujet die Fabel
Wenn es eine Pistole am Anfang einer Erzählung gibt
Mach mich Töte mich Sterbe mich

Oder noch besser gib mir die Briefe zurück.

Semiotik

Im letzten Gedicht aus diesem Zyklus —
wenn du und ich es schaffen, dort anzukommen —
werden wir an einem regnerischen Tag die Autoroute du soleil überqueren.
Das wird in den Neunzigern geschehen, am Ende des Jahrhunderts,
wenn der Kommunismus schon den besseren Teil der Menschheit erfaßt haben müßte,
die wunderbaren Männer und besonders Frauen von Ivan Efremov
müßten aus dem „Andromedanebel" herabgestiegen sein
und auf der wie ein betäubter Tiger gebändigten Erde schreiten
unter flammenden Himmeln über Trassen zu den Quantillionen und Quintillionen.

Andromeda wird in diesem möglichen Gedicht in Form eines Hotels erscheinen,
mit einer Sternkarte im Foyer.
Auf der Autobahn der Sonne wird es dämmrig sein
unter den üppigen orangenen Lampen Belgiens,
und der Mann, der das Auto fährt, wird in irgendeiner Sprache sagen meine Liebste
und wird seine Hand zwischen die Beine der Frau stecken, ohne sie zu fragen,
und die Frau neben ihm wird antworten mein Liebster, aber wird in ihrer Sprache denken

Hure, Flittchen, Schengener Fotze.

Sie wird ihn auch anfassen, wo sie will,
und er wird sich auch denken, was er will.
Im übrigen wird ihr Verlangen nach ihm nichts daran ändern,
wie sie über die Männer denkt.
In Wirklichkeit werden sie beide Frauen sein,
oder sie werden beide Männer sein, schwule Schwestern,
sie wird sein butch sein, er wird ihre femme sein,
gender trouble: she likes her girls to be boys.
Ihre Körper werden ständig in ihr Gegenteil katapultieren,
ohne daß noch jemand wüßte, was das Gegenteil ist,
wegen ihrer strengen Verurteilung werden
die Richtungen der Welt diese Funktionen auf sich nehmen müssen.

Ende des Jahrhunderts, fin de siecle, the end mit einem Wort Schluß, Ende,
während wir auf englisch kommen, ist das orgastische Ende auf bulgarisch,
in Augenblicken der Ekstase wird er sagen hurt me, kill me,
in Augenblicken der Ekstase wird sie sagen das Schönste ist daß du mich nicht verstehst
das Schönste ist daß Verliebte sich noch nicht einmal an ihren Wunden und blauen Flecken berühren
das schönste ist daß die Dichtung keine Grenzen überschreitet nicht mal ihre eigenen
das Schönste ist daß sie niemand mehr liest das Schönste ist daß sie die spiralförmige Galaxis
ohne Punkte und große Buchstaben an die fernen Ränder des Unmöglichen bringt
und uns auf unseren Autobahnen an unseren Grenzen läßt
damit einige sie überqueren andere an ihnen warten dritte weiterkriechen
unter ihnen unter den orangenen Lampen unter den Lastwagen
unter der Europäischen Union selbst. Das ist das Schönste my love amore mio
auf der autoroute du soleil.
Bei einbrechender Dunkelheit werden sie von der autoroute der Sonne abbiegen,
auf unbeleuchtetem Weg,
ganz eng unter nackten Bäumen, verwurzelt in der Zeit vor den Autobahnen.
Ein trockenes Blatt wird vor den Scheinwerfern vorbeifliegen —
zusammengerollt, von den Schatten vergrößert.

Eine Kröte — wird er sagen. Eine Kröte!
Sie hatten sie als Aphrodisiakum benutzt.
Dann wird er sehen, daß es ein trockenes Blatt ist, was soll eine Kröte im Dezember.
Er wird auch sehen, daß sie gesehen hat, sie wird sehen, daß er
gesehen hat, er hat gesehen, daß sie gesehen hat, daß er gesehen hat.

Schweigend werden sie fortfahren.

Translated by Gabi Tiemann

Easy Writing

Miglena Nikolchina

This is the tale of two lovers
that one story splits
or more precisely of the conflict between Fable and Subject in one account
but also not it exactly, because the conflict in reality exists
between fable & fable
between subject & subject
between between and between

This is a story with many pistols, but
they all go off in other texts.

Do with me as you will says someone
perhaps she? Perhaps he?

We start from the beginning.

"Easy Breathing" is one narrative by Bunin.[1]
"'Easy Breathing'" is an essay by Vygotsky about the story by Bunin

---

1 Sometimes translated as "Gentle Breathing," Ivan Bunin's 1916 story is about Olga Meschersky, a lively and carefree schoolgirl. Olga is entangled with two men and ultimately murdered by one of them; the diary entry about one man is a spur to the other's jealousy. The story is told retrospectively, through the memories of those who knew her. One of them, the schoolteacher referenced in the poem, remembers overhearing Olga talking about her father's "funny old books," which praised "gentle breathing" as a feature of female beauty and good behavior. (Translator's note.)

“‘“Easy Breathing”’” is an epistolary poem about two lovers who read “Easy Breathing”
“‘Easy Breathing’”
“‘“Easy Breathing”’”
“‘“‘“‘“‘“
”’”’”’”’”’

First Letter. She to him:
She breathes easy, he shoots her.

Second Letter. He to her:
The icky old man kisses her through the silk hankie,
she laughs. He shoots her.

Third Letter:
The old man is not so old, is not that disgusting.
she kisses him through the silk hankie, as if he were someone else.
as if he didn’t have a beard.
She masters the Secret of Ease.

Fourth Letter:
She shows him what she wrote in her diary
he shoots her.
The secret of ease is shooting
the easy shot.

Fifth Letter:
She writes about him, he shoots her.

Bunin writes! Bunin writes!

He writes and shoots her he
reads and shoots her.

But what is the Fable? What is the Subject?
the subject breathes easy the fable dies

easy breathing is the storyteller's art

Listen while I catch my breath

The schoolteacher prefers the air
she once breathed
Aprilwind.

Man and Air—there isn't such an "and"
she breathes the men how she sucks air no they
don't let them breathe the way one inhales
sometimes they have beards, sometimes pistols
So return to where there's breathing
where love is breathed

Anyway do with me as you will

Do with me as you will
Because I want you to do
Because I want you to want
Such is the subject of the fable
When there's a pistol at the beginning of the tale
Make me kill me death me

Or even better give back my letters

Semiotic

In the last poem of this cycle—
if you and I manage to get there—
we will cross the Autoroute du Soleil on a rainy day.
It will have happened in the '90s at the end of the century,
when communism should already have captured the better part of humanity,
Ivan Efremov's wonderful men and especially women ascended from

Andromeda Nebula[2] and walk the tamed Earth like a stunned tiger[3]
under skies aflame with routes to the quadrillions[4]

Andromeda will appear in this possible poem in the form of a hotel,
with a Starmap in the foyer.
On the Autobahn the sun will gloam
under the ample orange lamps of Belgium,
and the man, who drives the car, will in some language, or other, say my Most Beloved
and will stick his hand between the woman's legs, without asking,
and the woman beside him will answer my Most Beloved, but in her language will think
whore, slut, Schengener cunt.

She will also touch him, where she wants,
and he'll also think what he will.
Besides her desire for him won't change anything,
what she thinks about men.
In reality they'll both be women,
or they'll both be men, gay Sisters,
she'll be his butch, he'll be her femme,
Geschlechterzoff: Sie möchte, dass ihre gals will be guys.[5]
Their bodies will constantly catapult towards their opposites,
without anyone knowing, what the opposite is,
they think what they think, so the world has its way.

End of the century, fin de siecle, finito with a word ending, End,
as we come to English, the orgasmic ending is in Bulgarian,

---

2 Utopian novel (1957) by Soviet scientistic and science fiction writer Ivan Efremov, 1908–1972. (Translator's note.)

3 The Earth is compared to a stoned or drugged tiger. This is a reference to Stanislaw Lem's science fiction novel *Return from the Stars*. (Author's note.)

4 This is a reference to Ivan Karamazov's conversation with the devil about the distance it will take walking to paradise. (Author's note.)

5 Reference to Judith Butler's *Gender Trouble*: there is a sentence there, "I like my boys to be girls." Here it is reversed. (Author's note.)

in moments of Ecstasy he'll say tu mir weh, töte mich,
in moments of Ecstasy she will say sweetest[6] of all is you don't understand me
sweetest of all is that lovers not even once their wounds & blue bruises touch
sweetest of all is that poetry crosses no boundaries not even its own
sweetest of all is no one reads it anymore
sweetest of all is the spiriform galaxy
without periods and capital letters takes us to the far edge of impossible and
onto our motorways at our borders
so that some can cross others wait at them third crawl underneath them
under the orange lamps under the trucks
under the European Union itself.
That's the Sweetest of all meine Geliebte amore mio on the autoroute du soleil.

As darkness descends they will turn off the autoroute du soleil, onto a narrow unlit path
under naked trees, rooted in a time before highways.
A dry leaf will fly in the headlights curled up, magnified by shadows.
A toad—he'll say. A toad!
They use them as an aphrodisiac.

Then he'll see it's a leaf, not a toad in December.
He'll also see that she saw, she'll see that he
saw he saw that she saw, that he saw.

In Silence they will continue.

Translated by Marco Schindelmann and Alisa Slaughter

---

6 To κάλλιστον, "the most beautiful thing." Reference to Sappho 16 L.-P. Ann Carson, among others, translates it like this. (Author's note.)

Легке писання

Міглена Нікольчина

Це історія двох закоханих
розділених оповіддю
а точніше конфліктом між фабулою і сюжетом
в оповіді
але це теж не зовсім точно, бо насправді
конфлікт
між фабулою і фабулою
між сюжетом і сюжетом
між між і між
Це історія з багатьма пістолями, але всі вони
гримлять в інших текстах.
Роби зі мною, що хочеш, каже хтось
вона? він?

Почнемо спочатку.
„Легке дихання“ — оповідання Буніна.
„„Легке дихання““ — есе Л. С. Виготського про оповідання Буніна.
„„„Легке дихання“““ — це епістолярна поема
про двох закоханих.
які читають „Легке дихання“
„„Легке дихання““
„„„Легке дихання“““

„„„„„„„„„„„„„„„
“““ “““ “““ “““ ““

Перший лист. Вона до нього:
Вона дихає легко, він стріляє в неї.

Другий лист. Він до неї:
Гидкий старий цілує її через хустинку,
вона сміється. Він стріляє в неї.

Третій лист:
Старий не такий вже й старий, не такий вже й гидкий,
вона цілує його крізь хустинку, наче він хтось інший
ніби не має бороди.
Вона володіє секретом легкості.

Четвертий лист:
Вона показує йому запис про гидкого старого в щоденнику,
він стріляє в неї.
Секрет легкості у стрільбі,
легкий постріл.

П'ятий лист:
Вона пише, він стріляє в неї.

Бунін пише. Бунін пише!

Він пише і стріляє в неї
Він читає і стріляє в неї

Але що є фабулою? що сюжетом?
сюжет дихає легким диханням смерті фабули
Легке дихання — це мистецтво оповідача
Почуй, як я вдихну!

Чоловік і повітря — між ними немає „і"
вона дихає чоловіками, як вдихає повітря
а от вони, коли вдихають повітря, не дихають
іноді вони мають бороди, іноді пістолі

вона мусить повернутися туди, де дихають
туди, де дихають коханням.

І все ж роби зі мною, що хочеш
Роби зі мною, що хочеш
Тому що я хочу, щоб ти робив
Тому що я хочу, щоб ти хотів
Таким є сюжет фабули
Якщо на початку оповіді є пістоль
Змусь мене Вбити Вбий мене
Або краще поверни мені листи

Семіотичне

В останньому вірші цього циклу —
якщо ми з тобою зможемо туди потрапити —
в дощовий день ми перетнемо Autoroute du soleil.
Це станеться в дев'яностих, на зламі століть,
коли комунізм мав би охопити
кращу частину людства,
прекрасні чоловіки і особливо жінки Івана Єфремова
повинні були зійти з туманності Андромеди
і ступити на ручну, як тигр під наркотою
землю,
під небом, що палає шляхами у квадрильйони
і квінтильйони кроків.

Андромеда з'явиться в цьому можливому
вірші у вигляді готелю,
із зоряною мапою у вестибюлі.
Від численних помаранчевих ламп Бельгії на автостраді
меркне сонце
і чоловік за кермом авта скаже якоюсь
мовою кохана моя
і просуне руку між ніг жінці не

не питаючи її
і жінка поруч з ним відповість коханий мій, але
думатиме своєю мовою

курва, шльондра, шенгенська путана.

Вона також буде торкатися його, де захоче
і він так само думатиме власною мовою.
Тож її потяг до нього нічого не додасть
до того, що вона думає про чоловіків.
Насправді вони обидва будуть жінками
або обоє будуть чоловіками, ошаленілими лесбійками,
вона буде його butch, він буде її femme,
gender trouble: she likes her girls to be boys,
їхні тіла будуть постійно катапультуватися в
протилежність,
при цьому ніхто вже не знатиме, що таке протилежність,
це суворо засуджується,
саме тому ці функції будуть керуватися
напрямками світу.

Кінець століття, fin de siècle, the end, одним словом, кінець,

кінець,

в той час як англійською йдемо, болгарською
кінчаємо,
в моменти екстазу він скаже
hurt me, kill me

в моменти екстазу вона скаже
найкраще те, що ти мене не розумієш
найкраще те, що коханці не торкаються
ран і синців одне одного

найкраще те, що поезія не перетинає жодних
кордонів навіть власних

найкраще що її вже ніхто не читає
найкраще що її спіральна галактика без крапок і великих літер
закидає нас на край
неможливого
і залишає нас на наших автострадах на наших
кордонах

одні перетинають їх, другі висять на них, треті
повзуть
під ними під помаранчевими лампами під вантажівками
під самою Європейською спільнотою. Ось що є
найкраще my love amore mio
auf der autoroute du soleil.

В сутінках вони з'їжджають з автостради на
неосвітлену дорогу,
геть вузьку під голими деревами, укоріненими в
часи, коли ще не було автострад.
Зів'ялий лист пролетить перед фарами —
зібганий, збільшений тінню.
Жаба, — скаже він. Бугриста жаба!
Її використовували для покращення потенції.

Потім він побачить, що це сухий листок, яка ще жаба у
грудні.
А ще він побачить, що вона побачила, вона побачить, що він
побачив, він бачить, що вона бачить, що він бачить.

Вони продовжать у мовчанні.

Translated by Andriy Lysenko

Ratni Neseser

Maša Kolanović

Do prije toga dana mislila sam da se takav zvuk može čuti jedino na aeromitingu kada avioni na nebu iza sebe ostavljaju plave, bijele i crvene dimne trake, a piloti izvode vratolomije nešto kao Tom Cruise u *Top Gunu*. Samo što su ti aeromiting Cruisevi toga dana nosili maslinaste uniforme Jugoslavenske narodne armije.

Ja nikada nisam bila na aeromitingu, ali je moj brat u šestom razredu išao na modelare pa ih je drug jednom tamo vodio za nagradu. A onda su odjednom prestali postojati takvi aeromitinzi, kao što u školi više nismo smjeli govoriti „Druže!" i „Drugarice!" Sve se presvuklo u nešto drugo. Na primjer riječi: drug, drugarica i zdravo u nastavnik, nastavnica i dobar dan. Svečano smo bili primljeni u pionire, ali nismo dočekali omladince. Titovu sliku u školi su zamijenili hrvatski grb i križ. Misa više nije bila u dvosobnom stanu u Bolšićevoj, nego u holu naše škole, a naša se škola više nije zvala OŠ Branko Ćopić, nego OŠ Otok s kojom više nismo išli na izlet u Kumrovec ili Pionirski grad, nego u posjet dvorcima Hrvatskog zagorja. Većina prijatelja koji su se zvali Saša, Bojan ili Boro naglo su se odselili. Na svim jugićima nestalo je ono prvo slovo Y, a mnogi su na zvijezdu visokih starki zalijepili šahovnicu. U obrani časti prestali smo se zaklinjati na Titov ključić, u gumi-gumiju više nismo igrali Rade Končar kad smo pomoću zvijezde s jedne strane lastika prelazili na drugu. Ipak, možda je najgore bilo onim tipovima koji su imali tetovažu JNA plus neka godina.

Još u vrijeme tih aeromitinga, brat i ja imali smo našu malu uvjetnu družinu. Uvjetnu jer je uglavnom on dirigirao i mogao ju je raskinuti i opet sazvati kad god bi to poželio. A ja sam pristajala na sve jer sam pošto-poto htjela biti u blizini njega i njegovih prijatelja. Neki od njih su mi se zapravo i jako sviđali, mada sam uvijek znala da me oni uopće ne primjećuju i da pričaju o nekim tamo zgodnim curama iz svoje generacije, dok sam ja bila ošišana na gljivu i još k tome u stvarno jadnoj i nesvjetlucavoj odjeći od samta koju su mi uporno šivale mama i baka. Brat se u to vrijeme zanimao za raznorazne knjige o oružju i avionima koje mi je u trenucima dobre volje i nedostatka boljeg društva tumačio. Polikarpov I-16, Henšel HS 126 A-1, Meseršmit Bf 109E i još mnoge iz *Ilustrovane istorije vazduhoplovstva* i neke ultramoderne iz jedne knjige na engleskom. Premda u tim slikama nikada nisam pronalazila toliko toga zanimljivog kao on, bilo je i nekih ok stvari. Sjećam se jednog američkog aviona koji je imao oslikanu njušku kao morski pas. Brat je znao sve o avionima, oružju, vojskama. Meni je jedino bio ok taj morski pas avion i to da me brat ponekad podrazumijeva za svog prijatelja.

Uglavnom. Kada je taj zvuk aviona bio tako snažan i toliko blizu, bilo mi je jasno što je to zvuk s aeromitinga na kojem nikada nisam bila. Samo to zapravo i nije baš bilo ono što mi je prvo palo na pamet kada su tog popodneva prošla dva aviona iznad nas koji smo se to poslijepodne igrali pred zgradom. Zapravo, blago rečeno. Sutra je trebao biti prvi dan škole i bili su to zadnji trenuci igranja na kanalizacijskim šahtovima ispred zgrade jer će se već idućih tjeskobnih jesenskih popodneva trebati pisati domaće zadaće, počet će muzička, a ja ću morati vježbati klavir i učiti za *solfeggio* da ne osramotim mamu i tatu pred nastavnicom Milićkom. Kada su ti avioni proletjeli tik iznad naših glava, uhvatio me strah kakav sam prije toga dana osjetila jedino kada je drugarica, odnosno nastavnica, ispitivala geometriju listajući imenik i zadržavajući se negdje blizu slova K. Zapravo, osjećaj te nedjelje je bio mnogo strašniji. Svi smo istog trena pobjegli jer nas je potjerala teta Munjeković s četvrtog kata, a već su tako i tako sve glave susjeda bile na prozorima pa sam vidjela i maminu kako se dere neka smjesta dođem doma, što bih ja i bez njenog poziva učinila. Išli smo pješke, a ne liftom kao kad bismo se vraćali s igranja. Cijelo stubište bilo je uskomešano, a ja sam dok si rekao keks stigla do petog kata i srce mi je lupalo tako jako da sam mislila da ću dobiti infarkt, isti onaj za koji mi je mama rekla da ću dobiti ako popijem šalicu crne kave na eks.

Mama i tata su bili ozbiljni i nemirni, ne onako uobičajeno kao kada bi se svađali ili vikali na nas zbog nečega. U stanu su istovremeno bili upaljeni radio i televizija na kojima su bile vijesti. I dok su se na televiziji vidjeli neki neobrijani ljudi na barikadama i neki manje neobrijani ljudi ispod šahovnice s doktorom Franjom Tuđmanom na čelu, oglasila se sirena za zračnu uzbunu. Moja prva sirena za oglašavanje zračne opasnosti u životu. Do tada sam čula samo onu za Druga Tita kad smo se svi morali ukipiti u isti tren, bez obzira u kojem nas položaju ona zatekla. Stanje u stanu je tada doživjelo kulminaciju: tata je spuštao rolete, mama otišla isključiti plin, a brat sakriti krletku s papigom na neko mjesto udaljeno od prozora. Meni je srce opet lupalo kao u onom tobožnjem infarktu. Tata je onda rekao mami neka ponese stvari koje su već nekoliko dana bile spremljene u torbi smještenoj u predsoblju. Ja sam također brzo otišla po svoje stvari jer sam na sve ovo zapravo bila na neki način spremna.

Čula sam kako mama i tata preko telefona pričaju zabrinutije sa svim našim rođacima, ne propuštaju se niti jedne vijesti, a te godine nismo išli na more nego svega par dana. Baka i nono su isto tako bili jako zabrinuti, a i sve plaže kod Zadra bile su poprilično puste i bilo je puno mjesta za odložiti ručnike i ostalu opremu za kupanje. Sve je vodilo prema trenutku koji, iako smo ga nekako očekivali, nije nimalo izgubio na strašnosti. Ipak, trebalo je ostati pribranim, kako je to govorio susjed Stevo koji se ipak nije odselio. Moje su stvari, iako ni mama ni tata za njih nisu znali, isto bile spremne. U koferić na Štrumfove spremila sam svoju najvredniju pokretnu imovinu, najvažnije stvari koje sam na smaku svijeta htjela imati uza se. Jer, ako bomba pogodi baš našu zgradu i sve postane zgarište iz kojeg će mjestimice sukljati vatra i crni dimovi, život neće izgubiti smisao ako čitava ostane moja Barbi u svom kričavo roza kompletiću s malim fluorescentnim limunima, ananasima i bananama, rozazelenom torbicom u obliku lubenice, sunčanim naočalama te otvorenim štiklicama koje najbolje pristaju uz tu kombinaciju. I ako se, naravno, pri tom ništa loše ne dogodi bilo kojem članu moje obitelji, rodbine i prijatelja iz razreda i ulaza. Ostaviti Barbi na milost i nemilost granatama značilo je biti hazarder, a sama je Barbi bila tek jedan dio mog malog ratnog nesesera. Jer što je Barbi bez svojih savršenih stvari kojih jednostavno mora imati u izobilju?! Najobičnija seljača iz Rukotvorina kakvih sam se i previše nagledala prije nego što je baš Ona jednog dana napokon pokucala na moja vrata, točnije kaslić. A bilo je to davno, prije cijele te gužve s avionima i sirenama. Ispočetka, mama mi nipošto nije htjela kupiti ovaj komadić plastičnog savršenstva, ali o njoj se pričalo, za nju se znalo, a neki su je već i prije mene imali. Na primjer, jedna Ana F. iz sedamnajstice. Gledali smo je svi iz mog ulaza. I premda je bila toliko mala, oh, vrlo se dobro vidjela ta platinasta kaubojka u njenim rukama. A ne samo vidjela. Na kanalizacijskom šahtu, na kojem su se igrale cure ispred sedamnajstice, jednostavno se osjetilo da je tamo nešto što nije s ovoga svijeta, nešto što je moralo pasti s neba. Ana je imala baš pravu Barbi koju joj je air-mailom poslala teta iz Amerike. Onu koja ima plavu kosu, koja može saviti koljena i uz koju se dobije puno puno stvari. A nećakinja Nede Ukraden je, pričalo se, imala čak pedeset takvih Barbika! Ljubomora nije prava riječ za to što smo osjećali svi mi koji tada nismo imali pravu Barbi. Da pravu. Jer postojale su raznorazne „barbi" od neke odvratne plastike. Nematelovi lažnjaci s napuhanim obrazima, nesavitljivim koljenima, loše sašivenom robicom, katastrofalnim cipelicama i koje se k tome uopće nisu zvale Barbi, nego Stefi, Barbare, Cyndy i kojekakvim glupim imenima. A ne imati pravu Barbi značilo je biti iskonski nesretan. Tu mračnu fazu pr. Br. prekinuo je moj stric Ivo iz New Yorka i poslao Barbi na moju adresu jer jednostavno nije htio dopustiti da njegova nećakinja u Jugoslaviji bude bez tog malog, ali važnog pokazatelja prestiža i blagostanja.

Stigla je tako jednog dana u kaslić koji smo otvorile mama i ja. Na mamu je barem u tom trenutku, unatoč njezinoj tobožnjoj nezainteresiranost, prešla moja Barbi groznica. Vidjela sam joj to u očima. I doista je zbog toga ne smatram manje karakternom osobom jer ostati ravnodušan pred Barbi može samo netko tko je u najmanju ruku slijep. Ta je groznica bila obilježena spoznajom da me od mojeg najžuđenijeg komadića plastike ikad dijeli samo tanka ovojnica smeđeg pakpapira, ne dajući mi ni naslutiti koja će biti moja prva i to prava Barbi. I kada sam ga odmotala, jednostavno nije moglo ispasti savršenije jer je moja prva Barbi ujedno bila i moja najdraža glumica, Crystal iz *Dinastije*! Kad bolje promislim, možda to i zapravo nije bila baš ta Crystal, ali nije ni važno jer sam ja zamislila kao da je to ona glavom i bradom. Kada sam otvorila kutiju i odriješila *Crystal Barbie* zaštitnih ovojnica, bio je to osjećaj kao da sam dotaknula malo božanstvo. Ali ovo je božanstvo bilo puno savršenije od svih onih debelih i nezgrapnih božica iz prapovijesti kojih sam se prije toga nagledala na svakojakim izložbama u Arheološkom, po kojima su me mama i tata navlačili radi stjecanja kulture već u najmlađoj dobi. Njezina svjetlucava, malom roza vrpcom strukirana haljinica, na kojoj su se prelijevale sve nijanse boja odjednom, isto takva boja oko vrata, mali prsten, naušnice, srebrene šljokičaste cipelice, četkica i češalj za kosu, miris svježe plastike . . . sve je bilo tako stvarno! Ona više nije bila nedostižan predmet koji sam prije toga vidjela samo u reklamama na satelitskoj, a koju sam toliko puta zamišljala igrajući se u mašti kao da je stvarno posjedujem. Sada sam ja prvi put u životu imala nešto zaista vrijedno.

Odlomak iz *Sloboštine Barbie*
Ilustracije: Maša Kolanović

Wartime Necessities

Maša Kolanović

Until that day I thought you could only hear such a sound at an air show, when the planes in the sky left blue, white, and red trails and the pilots performed breakneck stunts like Tom Cruise in *Top Gun*. Except on this particular day, all the Tom Cruises were wearing the olive-green uniform of the Yugoslav People's Army.

I'd never been to an air show, but in the sixth grade my brother enrolled in a plane-modeling class, and their comrade took them to one as a reward. Then suddenly the air shows ceased, just like we were no longer allowed to call our teachers "Comrade!" Everything was repackaged. Including the word "comrade," which was folded into "Mister" and "Miss." And while we'd lavishly been inducted into the Yugoslav Union of Pioneers, there was no pomp or circumstance when the time came for the upgrade in rank to the League of Socialist Youth. At school, Tito's portrait was replaced by the Croatian coat of arms and the crucifix. Mass was no longer held in a two-bedroom apartment off Bolšić Street but in our school lobby. Our school was no longer named Branko Ćopić Elementary after the Yugoslav writer but "Island Elementary," and we no longer went on field trips to the Yugoslav Pioneer City but to an ancient Croatian castle or some such thing up north. Most of my friends with newly out-of-fashion names—Saša, Bojan, and Boro—moved away overnight. All the little Yugo cars lost their Ys, while Converse high-tops gained a Croatian checkerboard taped over the star. We stopped swearing on our honor by Tito's "little key" (whatever that was) and dropped the Communist Partisan Rade Končar star trick from our jump-rope routines. And yet, maybe worst off were those guys with the dated "JNA" tattoos, for the now-obsolete Yugoslav People's Army.

Back in the air-show days, my brother and I had a little impromptu gang—"impromptu" because he called all the shots and summoned or dismissed us whenever he pleased. I complied with his every demand, desperate to share in the atmosphere of him and his friends, a few of whom I had crushes on, though I entertained no illusions that they'd ever even noticed me. I knew their attention was reserved for the hot girls in their grade. Me? My mushroom haircut participated as an accessory to one of a million pitiful, glitterless corduroy outfits that two generations of women (my mother and grandmother) relentlessly sewed for me. Anyway, back then, my brother had taken an interest in books about weapons and fighter jets, and, during rare moments of goodwill, and for lack of better company, he would talk me through them. The Polikarpov I-16, the Henschel HS 126A-1, the Messerschmitt Bf 109E, and many more from the *Ilustrovane istorije vazduhoplovstva (The Illustrated History of Aviation)*, along with a few ultramodern ones from a book in English. Even though I never found any of it nearly as interesting as he did, there was some decent stuff. Like that American plane with its snout painted to resemble a shark. My brother knew everything there was to know about planes, about weapons, armies, you name it. I could appreciate that shark plane, and moments when my brother considered me a friend.

When one day the planes became as loud as they did, it dawned on me what the air shows must have sounded like—albeit this wasn't the first thought to cross my mind that afternoon when two planes whizzed past a hair's breadth above our heads while we were playing in front of our apartment building. School was supposed to start the following day, so those were our last moments of joy on the raised sewage vent out front. The ensuing anxiety-ridden fall afternoons would be dictated by homework, music lessons, piano practice, and solfeggio to avoid embarrassing my mother and father in front of the music teacher, Ms. Milić. When the planes hissed past us, I was gripped by the kind of fear I'd felt when my comrade—when my *teacher*—randomly quizzed us on geometry, flipping through the roster and lingering near the Ks. As a matter of fact, the feeling that Sunday was much more terrifying. We scattered immediately because we were chased off by Ms. Munjeković from the fourth floor, although all the neighbors' heads had already popped up in the windows of their apartments, including my mother's, shrieking that I was to come inside this instant, which I would have done without her bold invitation. We used the stairs and not the elevator, like we usually would after we played. The whole building was in complete disarray, and I reached our fifth-floor apartment before you could say *cakes*, my heart pounding so hard I thought I would suffer a heart attack, the kind of aches my mother warned I'd have if I consumed black coffee.

My mother and father were straight-faced and agitated, but not like when they were fighting with each other or scolding us about something. Inside the apartment, the radio and television were both on and tuned to the news. And when a group of unshaven men appeared on screen standing along barricades, and other slightly less unshaven men were shown assembling under the Croatian checkerboard with Dr. Franjo Tuđman at the fore, an air-raid siren sounded. My first-ever air-raid siren. Until then, I'd only heard the one for Comrade Tito's death, which obligated everyone to freeze no matter what position it had caught you in. The state of affairs in our apartment now reached its culmination: my father was rolling down the shutters, my mother turning off the gas, my brother moving the birdcage away from the window. My heart began pounding again like in that would-be heart attack. Then my father was telling my mother to grab their suitcase, which had already been packed several days prior and had since stood at attention in the foyer. I likewise bolted to fetch my own things, because when midnight finally struck, I, too, was, in a sense, prepared.

Over the previous weeks, I'd heard my mother and father sounding increasingly anxious on the phone with our extended family as they squeezed out every shred of news, and that year we'd skipped vacationing on the coast but for a couple of days. My grandmother and nono in Zadar seemed equally worried, and all the beaches near them were relatively deserted (there'd even been plenty of space to lay out your towel). All roads had been leading to this moment, which, albeit anticipated, was no less horrifying. Nevertheless, we had to "remain collected," as one of our neighbors kept saying. (His name—Stevo—had recently grown out of fashion, but he surprisingly hadn't moved away.) All this is to say that my things, which neither my mother nor father knew anything about, were also prepared. In my little Smurfs suitcase, I packed away my most prized portable property, the most important heirlooms I wanted by my side if the world ended. Should our building be struck by a bomb and reduced to ashes, spewing flames and black smoke, life would still be worth living if my Barbie remained whole, wearing her flashy little pink outfit with its tiny fluorescent lemons, pineapples, and bananas; her pink-and-green watermelon-shaped purse; her sunglasses; and the open-toe heels that completed the look. And, fingers crossed, if nothing happened to any member of my immediate family, my distant relatives, or my friends from school and from our building. Leaving Barbie at the mercy of the shelling would have been a reckless gamble, and Barbie was merely one share of my wartime necessities. I mean, what was Barbie without her abundance of flawless belongings? She would be reduced to the plainest peasant girl from the Handicrafts store, and I had seen more than enough of those before the day arrived when *She* finally knocked on my door (to be precise, my mailbox). But that was long ago, long before all that business with the planes and the sirens. In the beginning, my mother had absolutely refused to buy me that sliver of plastic perfection, but she was talked about, she was known, and some, like one Ana F. from building #17, had even acquired her before I had. Everyone from our building had watched Her. Even though she was so small, oh, that platinum-blonde cowgirl was clearly visible in Ana's hands. And not just *visible*. On the raised sewage vent where the girls from #17 played, you could just feel there was something extraordinary present, something that must have fallen from the sky. Ana's aunt had sent her this real Barbie by airmail from America. The blonde who could bend her knees and came with a ton of accessories. Rumor had it that the folk singer Neda Ukraden's niece owned as many as fifty! Jealousy is not the right word to express the feelings that overcame those of us who didn't have a real Barbie. Yes, a real one. For the record, there was no shortage of wannabe Barbies made from abysmal varieties of plastic. Non-Mattel fakes with puffy cheeks, unbendable knees, poorly sewn clothes, and catastrophic shoes, who weren't even called Barbie, but Stefi, Barbara, Cyndy—a whole gamut of stupid names. Needless to say, not having a real Barbie meant being profoundly unhappy. My uncle Ivo from New York finally put an end to this dark Before Barbie Era and sent one to our home, because, unlike all the others, he simply couldn't let his niece in Yugoslavia be deprived of that small but important token of prestige and prosperity.

It was the dawn of a new day when she arrived in our mailbox, which my mother and I opened together. At least in that moment, despite her previous show of disinterest, my mother caught Barbie fever. I saw it in her eyes. And it honestly didn't make me think she was any less in charge, since you would have to be blind (at the bare minimum) to remain indifferent in Barbie's presence. This fever was marked by the realization that only a thin layer of brown wrapping paper stood between me and my most coveted piece of plastic, preventing me from even guessing which one would be my first Barbie—no less, my first *real* one. When I unwrapped the package, it simply couldn't have come out more perfectly, because my first Barbie was also my favorite tv character: Krystle Carrington from *Dynasty*! (On second thought, it might not have actually been that Krystle, since the box had "Crystal" written on it, but this detail was immaterial and I imagined it was Krystle in the flesh.) And when I opened the box and loosened Crystal Barbie from her protective restraints, it felt like I had come into physical contact with a deity. Only *this* deity was much more glorious than all those fat and clumsy prehistoric goddesses that had set my corneas ablaze, given my exposure to all sorts of exhibits at the Archaeological Museum my mom and dad hauled me through in the hope that I would acquire a "cultural sense" from a very young age. Oh, that shimmery little pink ribbon tied around her iridescent, waist-defined cocktail dress, with a matching shimmery pink at her neckline; her small ring; her earrings; her little silver sequined shoes; her hairbrush and comb; the scent of fresh plastic—it was all so real! She was no longer an unattainable object in commercials on the satellite channels, inviting me to imagine for the umpteenth time that I was playing with her as if she were really mine. For the first time in my life, I had something that was truly valuable.

Excerpted from *Underground Barbie*
Translated by Ena Selimović
Illustrated by Maša Kolanović

Arról

Marcell Komor

Hommage á Lakner László

Amiről nem lehet	| beszélni |	arról hallgatni kell.[1]
	| speak |	
	| parler |	
	| sprechen |	
	| mówić |	
Amiről nem lehet hallgatni, arról	| говорити |	*kell*

1 Ludwig Wittgenstein, Logikai-filozófiai értekezés, 7. pont, utolsó mondat.

Thereof

Marcell Komor

Hommage á László Lakner

Whereof one cannot | speak | thereof one must be silent.[2]

| mówić |

| parler |

| sprechen |

| beszélni |

Whereof one

cannot be silent, thereof one must | говорити |

2 Ludwig Wittgenstein, Tractatus logico-philosophicus, paragraph 7, last sentence.

O tym

Marcell Komor

Hommage á László Lakner

O czym zaś nie można | mówić | o tym trzeba milczeć.[3]

| speak |

| parler |

| sprechen |

| beszélni |

O czym zaś nie

można milczeć, o tym trzeba | говорити |

3 Ludwig Wittgenstein: Tractatus logico-philosophicus (punkt 7, ostatnie zdanie)

Про те

Марсель Комор

Пам'яті Ласло Лакнера

Про те, про що не можна | сказати |, треба мовчати.[4]
| beszélni |
| speak |
| parler |
| sprechen |
| mówić |
Про те, про що не можна мовчати, треба | говорити |.

Translated by Andriy Lysenko

---

4 Див. Людвіг Вітгенштейн, Tractatus logico-philosophicus. Філософські дослідження, Київ, 1995, — с. 86 (пар. 7).

Надежда, 2022

Андрей Краснящих

> «<…> з неї тут же вилетіли усі нещастя, лиха, хвороби й занапастили весь рід людський. Перелякавшись, Пандора хутко зачинила кришку, але у скриньці залишилися тоді вже тільки одна *Надія*».
>
> «Історія давньогрецької літератури»

«У нас во дворе есть кот, он похож на Гитлера. У него такие же усы. Мы зовём его Путин».

Раз в день самолёт пролетает. Низко. Наш. Надя выскакивает из комнаты: «Не прилёт?» Никак не можем привыкнуть.

«Тут есть подвал? Он глубокий? И крепкий?»

Надя ждала десяти лет. Чтобы посмотреть фильмы ужасов. Многие подружки уже посмотрели «Кошмар на улице Вязов». Кто-то даже «Бивень». Кто-то даже «Сырое». Я отделывался, подсовывал ей «Охотников за привидениями», «Гремлинов», не такие уж хорроры. Её они не устраивали.

Десять Наде исполнилось 17 февраля. 19-го она праздновала с подружками в дельфинарии, впечатлений хватило на последующие дни. 24-го началась война.

В Полтаве, после месяца под бомбами в Харькове, Надя возобновила просьбы. Требования. Я решил, что уже можно. Надя хотела «Звонок». Он оказался нестрашным. «Звонок-2» был ещё хуже. Втихаря от меня посмотрела

«Кладбище домашних животных», о котором я ей рассказывал как о самом страшном ужастике своего детства. Смотреть его ей было нестрашно. Составили список. Я вспомнил, что мог. «Вой», «Телемертвецов», «Восставших из ада», «Экзорцист». «Сияние», «Поворот не туда», «Пятницу 13-е», «Крик». И ещё тридцать хорроров.

Боюсь, они её тоже не впечатлят. Мне нечего ей предложить. Период ужасов мы уже проскочили.

Теперь смотрим мультфильмы по «Нетфликс». «Морской монстр». Там тоже девочка лет десяти. Такая же розбышака. Пиратка. Гарпуны летают, как ракеты. Пушки — как «джавелины». На капитана, пошедшего войной, Надя говорит: «Как Путин». Наверное, таким теперь будет каждый мультфильм.

Меня кино тоже не впечатляет. До войны смотрел сериалы каждый день. Хорошие. Гордился, что разбираюсь. Знаю о новинках всё.

Делился с друзьями-сериаломанами. Писал о сериалах в глянец.

Перестал. Кино, сериалов с приходом войны не хотелось. Жена подписалась на «Нетфликс». Долго выискивал что бы. Впустую. Последний сезон «Лучше звоните Солу» хороший. Не затронул. Начал и бросил «1883», приквел «Йеллоустоуна».

Вместо кино — ленты новостей. Ни за одним сериалам так не следил. Но тут, как говорит мама, мы в кадре.

Прочитал в ленте, рассказываю Наде об игре, где детям дают призы за геолокацию. Спрашиваю, встречалось? Встречалось другое. В «Инстаграме» ей предложили 100 долларов за геолокацию наших военных мест. Она послала геолокацию Красной площади. Ответили: «Ждите». Не заплатили.

Моет машины на стоянке возле «Сільпо». Кто сколько даст. Гривен двадцать. «Многие девочки со двора так делают». Не знаю, как к этому относиться. Война всё поменяла, Надя быстро выросла.

Местные учат их просто жить, не боясь воздушных тревог и самолётов, зато у переселенцев к Путину особые счёты. Всё это перемешивается чудным образом.

Вернулся «Синий кит». Пятьдесят заданий, последнее — самоубийство. Первое — нарисовать красной ручкой сердце на запястье. Второе — синего кита на листе бумаги. Третье — его же на ноге. Четвёртое — прекратить общение со всеми. Пятое — пробежать вокруг своего дома несколько раз. Десятое — вырезать синего кита лезвием на руке. Тридцать девятое — перебежать через дорогу перед машиной.

Всё снимается на видео, отправляется на «Синий кит» в «Телеграме». В 4:20 утра.

Вернулся невовремя. В 4:20 или тревога, или спят. Дети пишут «Киту»: «Скажи: “Слава Украине!”» Он не отвечает. В 2018-м он был в «ВКонтакте».

Спрашиваю, играют ли дети во дворе в войнушку. Как мы в детстве. Есть ли «наши» и «русские» в этой игре. У нас были «наши» и «немцы».

Рисуем на воздушных шарах, оставшихся с праздника, эмоции. Страх, грусть, безнадёга. Справляется на раз. Усложняю: сомнение. Безразличие. Задумывается и находит. Узнаваемо. Задумываюсь и я. «Умиротворение». Задумывается надолго, потом быстро рисует зайца с крестиками на глазах и чем-то вроде банки в лапах. «?» — «Умер от варенья!»

Наде снова приснилось, что война закончилась. На этот раз ей сообщил Зеленский. Сам пришёл. «Открыл дверь и сказал». — «А дверь была не заперта?»

«Наверное, ты помнишь, мне приснилось, что Леночка к нам приехала? И она в тот же день приехала». — «Что война закончилась, тебе тоже снилось». — «Но тогда Зеленский не приходил».

«Надя, “Очаг” разрушили».

«!»

«Старшую школу».

«Эх».

В смысле — жаль, что не их, младшую. Но так они по старинке шутят. На самом деле: «Здравствуйте, Ирина Ивановна! Спасибо вам большое за эти 4 года школы! Вы были самым лучшим учителем! Вы очень хорошо преподавали и объясняли! Вы самый добрый учитель за всё это время! Спасибо вам большое за эти знания и годы! Скучаю по вам, очень надеюсь, что мы увидимся после войны!» Школа и есть учителя. У Ирины Ивановны дома нет. Разбомбило. Она в Киеве у подруги. «Здравствуйте, ребята. Будем встречаться онлайн по понедельникам в 11:00. Всё лето. Рассказывать друг другу, как мы, как дела. Хорошо?»

Никогда читать не любила. Приходится договариваться, заставлять. Выбираем, что может быть интересным. Не эта, не эта и не эта. «А какая?»

«Вот в Харькове у меня остались интересные».

Дома говорит по-русски. Все мы говорим на русском. Узнал, что во дворе они говорят на украинском. «Ну, на русско-украинском. На суржике». Попросила, чтобы дал ей украинскую книгу. Читает.

Наде бабушка передала баночку красной икры. «Ура!» Давно её не ела. «Это напоминает мне Харьков».

Скучает по своим игрушкам, оставшимся в Харькове.

Бабушка передала одну из них — «икеевскую» акулу.

Прижала к себе, понюхала. Говорит: «Харьковом пахнет».

Вчера снова была ракетная атака. В «Телеграме» выложили видео с пролетающей ракетой. Надя, посмотрев его, сказала, что, когда мы вечером 24 февраля шли через весь город к бабушке, она видела такую ракету, пролетавшую над нами. Мы не видели. И Надя до сих пор о ней не вспоминала, забыла накрепко.

Когда вернёмся домой, все вещи её придётся выкинуть или раздать. Выросла. И новые, подаренные на Новый, 2022-й год. И на день рождения 17 февраля. Через неделю мы ушли из дома налегке. Документы, коробка с кошкой. Думали, через день, через два вернёмся, всё окончится.

В «Телеграм»-канале о мёртвом котёнке. Лежащем в детской кровати. Сорок пять дней без хозяев. И фотография. Хоть бы не увидела.

А она знает. «Как хорошо, что мы Лотту взяли». И Лотте: «Мы тебя никогда не бросим». Думаю: «Как хорошо, что мы тебя вывезли. “В Україні від початку повномасштабного вторгнення загинуло 480 дітей”».

Лотта — в честь Лотты, «Дети с Горластой улицы» Астрид Линдгрен — любимая книжка, осталась дома. Я не читал. Её не было в моём детстве. В моём детстве были другие книги, фильмы. Теперь мои детские герои за войну со мной. Красная Шапочка за войну. Электроник тоже. Д'Артаньян, Харатьян. Говорят, Чебурашка — тайна русской души. У Нади другие фильмы, книги. Ей не нужно будет прощаться с мёртвыми сказочными героями. Её детство её не предаст.

У ребёнка небольшой жизненный опыт. Именно сейчас он формируется, и получается, формируется войной. За год войны Надя сильно изменилась, быстро выросла. Превратилась из ребёнка в подростка. Все дети Украины сильно повзрослели за время войны.

Ребёнок военного времени ест шаурму. Всё военное. На упаковке написано «За маму», «За тата» и «За ЗСУ», указано, за кого нужно сколько съесть. Шаурма — по-полтавски «шавуха» — вкусная.

Инсталляция, которую Надя сделала маме на день рождения. Лена ответила, что бы хотела в подарок: «Голову Путина». Материал — солёное тесто, гуашь, вычесанная кошачья шерсть. Флаг Украины — пластмассовая палочка — вставлен в уши. Лицо Путина удивлённое. Путин очень похож.

Нарисовала картину. Холст — сто гривен в социальном магазине. Углы потёрты. Нормальный бы стоил сто пятьдесят.

В подарок Ларисе, хозяйке квартиры. Пейзаж, людей нет, есть деревья. Дубы, кусты. Очень реалистичные. Очень реалистичные облака. Синее небо, красок не пожалела. Призрачные качели, дорога и что-то ещё, что относится к людям. Не хватило, наверное, краски.

В углу расписалась. Написала «Надежда». Поставила год: «2022».

«Пап, пап, а весной свет уже отключать не будут?»

«Нет. Сказали, что всё, ситуацию выровняли. Хотя это ж Россия. Что им стоит новую пакость придумать».

«Да, я знаю. Но нужно ж чему-то радоваться».

Да-да-да, именно дети. Дети и кошки — ключевые герои всей нашей истории. Для меня. Старики упираются, взрослые суетятся, дети и кошки воспринимают всё как есть, в системе своей жизни.

Фотографии Харькова. У кого на окне стоит икона, у кого-то наклеено «НАХУЙ». Чаще всего окон нет: забиты фанерой.

Я спокоен. До войны нервничал по всякому поводу. Лекции. Поездки. Работа. Меня правили в «Харькове — что, где, когда» — переживал и злился. Днями, неделями накручивал себя. Хотел мести и справедливости. Перед лекцией начинал волноваться за день. За час до лекции всего трясло, поднималось давление, тошнило, кружилась голова.

Месяц под бомбами меня вылечил. Я находился в ступоре, жутко боялся. Потом страх утих.

Сегодня я ни о чём не волнуюсь. Волнуюсь за родителей, проблемы на работе меня не трогают. Читаю лекции на украинском, импровизируя на каждом шагу. На жутком суржике. Меня это не беспокоит. Мои лекции на русском, листы бумаги, остались дома. Я здесь, я выжил, меня не заботит ни будущее, ни деньги. Университет не выплатил отпускные, сократил на полставки, не дал зарплаты за полсентября, отправил за мой счёт на каникулы. Мне всё равно. Я пробовал возмутиться, довести себя до кондиции, мне это неинтересно. Мне интересно просто жить. Я радуюсь кошке, которая рада мне и мурчит. Она тоже долгое время была в ступоре, не могла ни есть, ни общаться. Мне нравится ходить по улицам, видеть людей. Моя дочь взрослеет, покрасила волосы, коротко подстриглась. Похожа на Алису из «Гостьи из будущего». («Алиса, в будущем весело?» — «Да просто ахуеть».) Мне приятно думать, что я дожил. Ей нравится школа, уроки, но она не признается в этом. Я слышу, она отвечает в соседней комнате, вижу — готовится к урокам. На украинском ей задали написать легенду. «Одного разу на місто і державу, в якій воно знаходиться, напала сусідня країна. Вона пускала ракети, стріляла з танків, бомбила літаками. І всі діти цього міста змушені були спуститися в підвали та льохи. Вони сиділи тиждень, два, три, місяць та більше. Без сонця та вуличних ігор ставали сумнішими і сумнішими і ні з ким не хотіли спілкуватися. Ані з батьками, ані з друзями. Але кожна дитина мала по кішці. Пухнасті, м'які, вони муркотіли дітям, заспокоювали їх. Діти розмовляли лише з кішками. Коли війна закінчилася і діти вийшли з льохів, виявилося, що кожна дитина мала по кішці, яка врятувала її. Про це дізналися всі городяни і поставили кішкам пам'ятник і по всьому місту миски, в які щоранку наливали молоко. З того часу традиція збереглася і кішок усі поважають».

Кошка кусает мне руку, хочет играться. Я с ней играюсь.

Nadezhda, or Hope, 2022[1]

Andrei Krasniashchikh

> . . . all calamities, misfortunes, and diseases flew out at once and plagued the entire human race. Pandora, frightened, quickly shut the lid, yet remaining in the box was but one: Hope.
>
> *The History of Ancient Greek Literature*[2]

"There's a cat in our courtyard, he looks like Hitler, he has the same kind of whiskers. We'll call him Putin."

Once a day a plane flies by. Close to the ground. It's one of ours.

Nadia leaps out of her room. "It's not coming towards us, is it?"

We cannot get used to this.

"Is there a cellar here? Is it deep? And sturdy?"

Nadia waited ten years to watch horror films. A lot of her friends had already seen *A Nightmare on Elm Street.* One had even seen *Tusk.* Another *Raw.* I stalled, I slipped her *Ghostbusters, Gremlins,* not real horror films. She wasn't satisfied.

---

1 The name "Nadezhda" means "hope" in Russian. "Nadia" is a diminutive version of "Nadezhda." (Translator's note.)

2 This text is translated from Russian, but the epigraph and the daughter's assignment are in Ukrainian in the original and translated from Ukrainian. (Editors' note.)

On February 17th Nadia turned ten. On the 19th she celebrated with friends at a dolphinarium, her impressions lasted for the next few days. On the 24th the war began.

In Poltava, after having spent a month under shelling in Kharkiv, Nadia appealed again. She insisted. It was now okay, I decided. She wanted to see *The Ring*—it turned out not to be frightening. *The Ring Two* was even more disappointing. In secret, unknown to me, she watched *Pet Sematary,* which I'd described to her as the most terrifying horror movie of my childhood. She didn't find it frightening. We made a list. I remembered what I could: *The Howling, Video Dead, Hellraiser, The Exorcist, The Shining, Wrong Turn, Friday the 13th, Scream*. And thirty more horror films. I worry that these, too, won't make an impression on her. I have nothing to offer her. The time of horrors is already behind us.

Now we watch cartoons on Netflix. *The Seabeast*. The girl in the cartoon is also ten years old. She's a mischief-maker, a girl-pirate. Harpoons fly like rockets. Guns like Javelins. About the captain who went off to war, Nadia says, "like Putin." All cartoons will probably be like this now.

On me, too, cinema makes no impression. Before the war I watched serials every day. Good ones. I took pride in following what was going on, in keeping up with everything new. I shared my thoughts with my serial-addict friends. I wrote about the serials in glossy magazines.

I've stopped watching. With the arrival of the war, movies and tv shows lost their appeal. My wife signed up for Netflix. For a long time I looked around for something or other. To no avail, it was futile. The final season of *Better Call Saul* is good—but it didn't touch me. I started and abandoned *1883,* the prequel to *Yellowstone*. I haven't followed a single serial. Instead of films there are newsfeeds. Here, though—as my mother says—we are the ones captured on the screen.

I read a newsfeed, I tell Nadia about a game where children get rewards for geolocation. I ask her: have you come across this? She's come across something else. On Instagram she was offered 100 dollars for the geolocation of our military sites. She sent the geolocation of Red Square. They answered: "Just hold on." They never paid.

Nadia washes cars in the parking lot next to Silpo, the local store. How much will people pay? Maybe twenty hryvnia.

"A lot of the girls from our courtyard are doing this."

I don't know what to think about that. The war has changed everything. Including Nadia. She's grown up quickly.

The locals teach them to just live, without being afraid of air raid sirens and planes, while the displaced persons have their own accounts to settle with Putin. It all mixes together wonderfully.

Blue Whale has returned.[3] Fifty tasks, the final one being suicide. The first—draw a heart on your wrist with a red pen. The second—draw a blue whale on a piece of paper. The third—draw it on your leg. The fourth—cease to communicate with everyone. The fifth—run around your home several times. The tenth—carve a blue whale with a blade on your hand. The thirty-ninth—run across the street in front of a car.

Everything is filmed, the videos are to be sent to Blue Whale on Telegram, at 4:20 am. It's an inopportune moment for Blue Whale to have returned. At 4:20 am either people are sleeping or there's an air raid siren. Children write to Blue Whale: "Say '*Slava Ukraini*! Glory to Ukraine!'" Blue Whale doesn't answer. In 2018 he was on VKontakte.

I ask whether kids are playing war games in the courtyard, like we did when we were young. Whether it's "us versus the Russians" in these games. In my childhood it was "us versus the Germans."

We make drawings on balloons left over from a celebration. We draw emotions: fear, sadness, hopelessness. Nadia manages well for a while. I make it more complicated: Uncertainty. Indifference. She thinks it over and figures it out. It's recognizable.

I, too, am thinking it over.

"Appeasement."

---

3 Blue Whale or Blue Whale Challenge is a suicide game consisting of some fifty, increasingly ominous, tasks. The game, targeting vulnerable adolescents, became a social media phenomenon; it seems to have originated in Russia around 2016. (Translator's note.)

She thinks for a long time, then, quickly, draws a hare with crosses on its eyes and something like a jar in its paws.

"...?"

"He died of peas!"

Nadia dreamt again that the war ended. This time Zelensky brought her the news. He came himself, in person.

"He opened the door and said it."

"The door wasn't locked?"

"You remember when I dreamt that Lenochka came to visit us? And she came that same day."

"You also dreamt that the war ended."

"But that time Zelensky didn't come."

"Nadia, they destroyed the 'Hearth.'"

"..!"

"The high school."

"Oh..."

In the sense of, a pity it's not their school, the elementary school. But that's just their way of joking. The reality is this: *"Hello Irina Ivanovna! Thank you so much for these four years of school! You were the best teacher ever! You explained things so well! The whole time you were the nicest teacher! Thank you so much for what you taught us and for these years! I miss you, and I really hope we'll see each other after the war!"*

School is the teachers. Irina Ivanovna is homeless. Her home was bombed. She's staying with a friend in Kyiv.

"Good morning, students! We'll meet online on Mondays at 11 am. All summer. And tell one another how we're doing and what's going on. Okay?"

Nadia has never liked to read. I have to bargain, force her. We choose what might be interesting. Not this book, or this one. And not this one.

"Which one then?"

"The interesting books stayed in Kharkiv."

At home she speaks in Russian. We all speak in Russian. I learned that in the courtyard they speak in Ukrainian.

"Well, in Russian-Ukrainian. In *surzhik*."

She asked me to give her a book in Ukrainian. She's reading it.

Nadia's grandmother gave her a jar of red caviar.

"Yay!"

She hasn't eaten caviar in a long time.

"It reminds me of Kharkiv."

She misses the toys she left behind in Kharkiv. Her grandmother brought her one of them, a shark from IKEA.

She hugged the shark and sniffed it.

"It smells like Kharkiv," she says.

Last night there was another rocket attack. A video of a flying rocket was posted on Telegram. When she saw it, Nadia told us that on February 24th, in the evening when we crossed the whole city to get to where her grandmother lived, she'd seen a rocket like this flying above us. We hadn't seen it. And until now Nadia had never mentioned it, she'd forcibly forgotten.

When we return home, all her things will have to be thrown out or given away. She's grown up. The new things, too, given to her for the holidays, and for her birthday on February 17. A week afterwards we left home traveling light: documents, a box with a cat. We thought we'd return in a day or two, that it would all be over.

On Telegram there's a story about a dead kitten. It was lying in a child's bed. Forty-five days without its owners. And a photograph. At least Nadia didn't see the photograph.

But she knows.

"What a good thing that we took Lotta."

And to Lotta: "We'll never abandon you."

I think: "*What a good thing that we took you away from there.*"

"Four hundred and eighty children have been killed in Ukraine since the beginning of the full-scale invasion," the media informs us.

Lotta—in honor of Lotta, *The Children of Noisy Village* by Astrid Lindgren, her favorite book, was left at home. I've never read it. It didn't exist when I was a child. In my childhood we had different books, different films. Now my childhood heroes have turned against me, the stars of these films declaring themselves for war against Ukraine. Little Red Riding Hood. Elektronik, too. D'Artagnan, Kharatyan.[4] Cheburashka—they say—is the secret to the Russian soul.[5] Nadia has different films, different books. She will not be forced to break up with dead fairy tale heroes. Her childhood will not betray her.

A child has had limited life experience. She is being formed right now, and war, it turns out, is doing the forming. Nadia has changed so much during a year of war, she's grown up very quickly. She's been transformed from a child into an adolescent. All Ukrainian children have matured so much during the war.

Everything is about the war. A child is eating shawarma during wartime. On the packaging it says "For Mom," "For Dad," "For the Armed Forces of Ukraine," indicating how much needs to be eaten for whom. The shawarma—in Poltava slang, *shavukha*—tastes good.

Nadia created an installation for her mother on her birthday. Lena had told her what she wanted as a gift: "Putin's head." Materials: salt dough, gouache, combed cat fur. A Ukrainian flag—a plastic stick—inserted into the ears. Putin's face has a surprised look. It looks very much like Putin.

---

4 *About the Little Red Riding Hood* (Pro Krasnuiu Shapochku) is a 1977 Soviet film starring Yana Poplavskaya (b. 1967) as Little Red Riding Hood. Dmitry Kharatyan (b. 1960) is a Russian actor who appeared in many Soviet films in the 1980s. D'Artagnan is a character in the 1978 Soviet film *D'Artagnan and the Three Musketeers* (D'Artagnan i tri mushketera), based on the Alexandre Dumas novel. He was played by Russian actor Mikhail Boyarsky (b. 1949). Elektronik is the robot protagonist of *The Adventures of Electronic* (Prikliucheniia Elektronika), a Soviet science fiction miniseries for children popular in the 1980s. Elektronik was played by Vladimir Torsuev (b. 1966), whose twin brother, Iurii Torsuev, played Sergei, the boy who served as the model for Elektronik in the story. (Translator's note.)

5 Cheburashka is a fictional character created by the Soviet writer Eduard Uspensky in his 1965 children's book *Gena the Crocodile and His Friends*. (Translator's note.)

Nadia painted a picture. The canvas cost 100 hryvnia at a discount store. The corners were worn. It would have normally cost 150. A gift for Larisa, the owner of the apartment. A landscape, no people, trees. Oaks, bushes—very realistic. Very realistic clouds. A blue sky, she didn't spare the paint. Swings, a road and something else related to people are spectral. The paint must have been running out. In the corner she signed the painting. She wrote: "*Nadezhda*"—and the year: "*2022*."

"Dad? Dad, in the spring the lights won't be shut off?"

"No. They said it was over, the situation was under control. Although this is Russia—they'll come up with another nasty trick."

"I know. But we have to be happy about something."

Yes, yes, yes, namely, children have to be happy about something. Children and cats—the central heroes of our whole story. For me. The elderly are stubborn, adults fuss, children and cats accept everything as it is, taking it into the system of their life.

Photographs of Kharkiv. In someone's window an icon, in someone else's window the pasted words "GO FUCK YOURSELF."[6] Most often there are no windows; they're covered with plywood.

I'm calm. Before the war everything made me nervous. Lectures. Trips. Work. They revamped my texts in the journal *Kharkiv—Where, When, What*. I was unnerved, furious. For days, weeks I was overwrought. I wanted justice, and revenge. The day before a lecture I would start to get anxious. An hour before a lecture everything would tremble, my blood pressure would go up, I'd feel dizzy and sick.

A month under shelling cured me. I found myself in a stupor, terrified—and then the fear quieted down. Today I don't worry about any of this. I worry about my parents, problems at work don't touch me. I give lectures in Ukrainian,

---

6 On February 24, 2022 the Russian warship *Moskva* began an assault on Ukraine's Snake Island in the Black Sea. *Moskva* demanded that the small number of Ukrainian border guards there put down their weapons and surrender. One of them, Roman Hrybov, responded, "Russian warship, go fuck yourself!" (Russkii voennyi korabl', *idi nakhui*!) The phrase became a Ukrainian slogan and a rallying call for the resistance to the Russian invasion. (Translator's note.)

improvising at every step. In a terrible *surzhik*. It doesn't bother me. My lectures in Russian, the sheets of paper, have remained at home. I'm here, I've survived, I'm concerned neither about the future nor about money. The university didn't give me holiday pay, reduced my status to halftime, didn't pay my salary for half of September, sent me on unpaid vacation. It's all the same to me. I tried to be indignant, to work myself into a state, I'm uninterested. I'm just interested in living. I enjoy the cat, who enjoys me and who purrs. She, too, was in a stupor for a long time, unable to eat or socialize. I like to walk the streets, to see people. My daughter is growing up, she's dyed her hair and cut it short. She looks like Alisa in *Guest from the Future*.[7] (*"Alisa, will the future be fun?"—"Yeah, it will be fucking awesome."*) I enjoy the thought that I'm still alive. Nadia likes school, she likes her lessons, although she doesn't admit it. I listen as she gives answers in the next room, I see her preparing for her classes. For Ukrainian class, her assignment was to write a legend.

One day the city, and the state where the city was located, were attacked by a neighboring country. The neighboring country shot rockets, fired from tanks, bombed from airplanes. And all the children in the city were forced to go down into basements and cellars. They sat there for a week, two weeks, three weeks, a month and longer. Without sun and without playing outside they became sadder and sadder and didn't want to talk to anyone. Neither with their parents, nor with their friends. But each child had a cat. Furry, soft, the cats purred at the children, calming them down. The children only talked to the cats. When the war ended and the children came out of the cellars, it turned out that each child had a cat who'd saved them. Everyone in the city found out about this and built a monument to the cats and put bowls all over the city and poured milk into them every morning. Since that time the tradition has been preserved and cats are respected by everyone.

The cat nibbles my hand, she wants to play. So, I play with her.

Translated by Marci Shore

---

7 *Guest from the Future* is a Soviet science fiction television series for children that first aired in 1985. (Translator's note.)

Надія, 2022

Андрій Краснящих

> «<…> з неї тут же вилетіли усі нещастя, лиха, хвороби й занапастили весь рід людський. Перелякавшись, Пандора хутко зачинила кришку, але у скриньці залишилися тоді вже тільки одна Надія».
>
> «Історія давньогрецької літератури»[8]

«У нас на подвір'ї є кіт, він схожий на Гітлера. Має-бо такі ж вуса. Ми звемо його Путін».

Раз на день пролітає літак. Низько. Наш. Надя вискакує з кімнати: «Не приліт?» Ніяк не звикнемо.

«Тут є підвал? Він глибокий? Надійний?»

Надійка чекала десяти років. Щоб подивитися фільми жахів. Багато подружок уже переглянули «Кошмар на вулиці В'язів». А хтось ще й «Бивень», ба навіть «Сире». Я намагався маневрувати, підсовував їй «Мисливців за привидами», «Гремлінів», не такі вже й страшні. Її вони не влаштовували.

Десять доньці виповнилося 17 лютого. 19-го вона святкувала з подружками в дельфінарії, вражень вистачило на кілька наступних днів. 24-го почалася війна.

---

8 В оригіналі епіграф дається українською.

Вже у Полтаві, після місяця під бомбами в Харкові, Надя знову почала прохати. Вимагати. Я вирішив, що вже можна. Вона хотіла «Дзвінок». Він виявився нестрашним. «Дзвінок-2» виявись ще гіршим. Тишком-нишком від мене подивилася «Цвинтар домашніх тварин», про який я їй розповідав як про найбільш моторошний хорор свого дитинства. Дивитися його їй було нестрашно. Склали список. Я згадав, що міг. «Виття», «Телемерці», «Повсталі із пекла», «Екзорцист». «Сяйво», «Поворот не туди», «П'ятниця 13-те», «Крик». І ще тридцять назв.

Боюся, вони її теж не вразять. Мені нічого їй запропонувати. Період жахіть ми вже проскочили.

Тепер дивимося мультфільми по «Нетфлікс». «Морський монстр». Там теж дівчинка років десяти. Така ж розбишака. Піратка. Гарпуни літають, як ракети. Гармати — як «джавеліни». На капітана, який пішов війною, Надя каже: «Як Путін». Напевно, таким тепер буде кожен мультфільм.

Мене кіно теж не вражає. До війни щодня дивився серіали. Вартісні. Пишався, що розбираюся. Знаю про новинки все.

Ділився з друзями-серіаломанами. Писав огляди в глянець.

Припинив. Кіно, серіалів із приходом війни не хотілося. Дружина підписалася на «Нетфлікс». Довго вишукував, що б ... Даремно. Прекрасний останній сезон «Краще подзвоніть Солу». Не зачепив. Почав і кинув приквел «Єллоустоуна» — «1883».

Замість кіно — стрічки новин. За жодним серіалом так не стежив. Але тут, як каже мама, ми в кадрі.

Прочитав у стрічці, розповідаю Наді про гру, де дітям дають призи за геолокацію. Питаю, зустрічалося? Зустрічалося інше. В «Інстаграмі» їй запропонували 100 доларів за геолокацію наших військових місць. Вона надіслала геолокацію Красної площі. Відповіли: «Чекайте». Не заплатили.

Миє машини на стоянці біля «Сільпо». Хто скільки дасть. Гривень двадцять. «Багато дівчаток з подвір'я так роблять». Не знаю, як до цього ставитися. Війна все змінила, Надя швидко виросла.

Місцеві вчать їх просто жити, не боячись повітряних тривог і літаків, зате до Путіна у переселенців особливі рахунки. Усе це перемішується дивним чином.

Повернувся «Синій кит». П'ятдесят завдань, останнє — самогубство. Перше — намалювати червоною ручкою серце на зап'ясті. Друге — синього кита на аркуші паперу. Третє — його ж на нозі. Четверте — припинити спілкування з усіма. П'яте — пробігти навколо свого будинку кілька разів. Десяте — вирізати синього кита лезом на руці. Тридцять дев'яте — перебігти через дорогу перед машиною.

Усе знімається на відео, відправляється на «Синій кит» у «Телеграмі». О 4:20 ранку.

Повернувся невчасно. О 4:20 або тривога, або сплять. Діти пишуть «Киту»: «Скажи: "Слава Україні!"». Він не відповідає. У 2018-му він був у «ВКонтакте».

Запитую, чи грають діти у дворі у війнушку. Як ми в дитинстві. Чи є в цій грі «наші» і «росіяни». У нас були «наші» і «німці».

На повітряних кулях, що залишилися зі свята, малюємо емоції. Страх, смуток, безнадія. Жодних проблем. Ускладнюю: сумнів, байдужість. Замислюється і знаходить. Впізнавано. Тепер замислююсь я. «Умиротворення». Довго роздумує, потім швидко малює зайця з хрестиками на очах і чимось на кшталт банки в лапах. «?» — «Помер від варення!»

Наді знову наснилося, що війна закінчилася. Цього разу їй повідомив Зеленський. Сам прийшов. «Відчинив двері і сказав». — «А двері були не замкнені?»

«Напевно, ти пам'ятаєш, мені наснилося, що Оленка до нас приїхала? І вона того ж дня приїхала». — «Що війна закінчилася, тобі теж снилося». — «Але тоді Зеленський не приходив».

«Надю, "Очаг" зруйнували».

«!»

«Старшу школу».

«Ех».

У сенсі — шкода, що не їхню, молодшу. Але так вони тільки жартують. Насправді ж: «Здрастуйте, Ірино Іванівно! Спасибі вам велике за ці 4 роки школи! Ви були найкращим учителем! Ви дуже добре викладали і пояснювали! Ви найдобріший учитель за весь цей час! Дякую вам велике за ці знання і роки! Сумую за вами, дуже сподіваюся, що ми побачимося після війни!» Викладачі — оце й є школа. В Ірини Іванівни немає будинку. Розбомбило. Вона в Києві у подруги. «Здрастуйте, дітвора. Щопонеділка об 11:00 зустрічатимемось онлайн. Усе літо. Розповідатимемо одне одному, як ми, як справи. Добре?»

Ніколи не любила читати. Доводиться домовлятися, змушувати. Вибираємо, що може бути цікавим. Не ця, не ця і не ця. «А яка?»

«От у Харкові в мене залишилися цікаві».

Вдома говорить російською. Всі ми говоримо російською. Дізнався, що на подвір'ї вони говорять українською. «Ну, російсько-українською. Суржиком». Попросила, щоб дав їй українську книжку. Читає.

Бабуся передала Наді баночку червоної ікри. «Ура!» Давно її не їла. «Це нагадує мені Харків».

Сумує за своїми залишеними в Харкові іграшками. Бабуся передала одну з них — «ікеївську» акулу. Притиснула до себе, понюхала. Каже: «Харковом пахне».

Вчора знову була ракетна атака. У «Телеграмі» виклали відео з прольотом ракети. Надя його подивилась і сказала, що коли ми ввечері 24 лютого йшли через усе місто до бабусі, вона бачила над нами таку ракету. Ми не бачили. І Надя досі про неї не згадувала, забула наніц.

Коли повернемося додому, всі її речі доведеться викинути або роздати. Виросла. І нові, подаровані на Новий, 2022-й рік. І на День народження 17 лютого. Через тиждень ми пішли з дому без нічого. Документи, коробка з кішкою. Думали, за день-два повернемося, все закінчиться.

У «Телеграмі» про мертве кошеня. Лежить у дитячому ліжечку. Сорок п'ять днів без господарів. І фотографія. Хоч би не побачила.

А вона знає. «Як добре, що ми Лотту взяли». І Лотті: «Ми тебе ніколи не кинемо». Думаю: «Як добре, що ми тебе вивезли». «В Україні від початку повномасштабного вторгнення загинуло 480 дітей».

Лотта — на честь Лотти, «Діти з Горластої вулиці» Астрід Ліндгрен — улюблена книжка, залишилася вдома. Я не читав. Її не було в моєму дитинстві. У моєму дитинстві були інші книжки, фільми. Тепер мої дитячі герої за війну проти мене. Червона Шапочка за війну. Електронік теж. Д'Артаньян, Харатьян. Кажуть, Чебурашка — таємниця російської душі. У Наді інші фільми, книжки. Їй не доведеться прощатися з мертвими казковими героями. Її дитинство її не зрадить.

У дитини невеликий життєвий досвід. Саме зараз він формується, а отже, формується війною. За рік війни Надя сильно змінилася, швидко виросла. Перетворилася з дитини на підлітка. Всі діти України сильно подорослішали за час війни.

Дитина воєнного часу їсть шаурму. Все військове. На упаковці написано «За маму», «За тата» і «За ЗСУ», зазначено, за кого потрібно скільки з'їсти. Шаурма — по-полтавськи «шавуха» — смачна.

Інсталяція, яку Надя зробила мамі на день народження. Олена замовила подарунок: «Голову Путіна». Матеріал — солоне тісто, гуаш, вичесана котяча шерсть. Прапор України — пластмасова паличка — вставлений у вуха. Обличчя Путіна здивоване. Путін дуже схожий.

Намалювала картину. Полотно — сто гривень у соціальному магазині. Кути потерті. Нормальне б коштувало сто п'ятдесят. У подарунок Ларисі, господині квартири. Пейзаж, людей немає, є дерева. Дуби, кущі. Дуже реалістичні. Дуже реалістичні хмари. Синє небо, фарб не пошкодувала. Примарна гойдалка, дорога і щось іще, що відноситься до людей. Напевно, не вистачило фарби.

У кутку розписалася: «Надія». І рік: «2022».

«Тату, тату, а навесні світло вже не відключатимуть?»

«Ні. Сказали, що все, ситуацію вирівняли. Хоча це ж Росія. Що їм вартує нову капость придумати».

«Так, я знаю. Але потрібно ж чомусь радіти».

Так-так-так, саме діти. Дітлахи і кицьки — ключові герої всієї нашої історії. Для мене. Люди похилого віку впираються, дорослі метушаться, діти і кішки сприймають все, як є, в системі свого життя.

Фотографії Харкова. У когось на вікні стоїть ікона, у когось наклеєно «НАХУЙ». Найчастіше вікон немає: забиті фанерою.

Я спокійний. До війни нервував з кожного приводу. Лекції. Поїздки. Робота. Порізали статтю в «Харків — що, де, коли» — переживаю, злюся. Днями, тижнями себе накручую. Прагну помсти і справедливості. Перед лекцією починаю хвилюватися: як пройде день. За годину до лекції всього трясе, піднімається тиск, нудить, паморочиться в голові. Місяць під бомбами мене вилікував. Спочатку ступор, нестримний страх. Потім страх ущух.

Нині я ні про що не хвилююся. Хіба що за батьків, а от проблеми на роботі геть не зачіпають. Читаю лекції українською, імпровізуючи на кожному кроці. Моторошним суржиком. Мене це не турбує. Мої записи лекцій російською залишилися вдома. Я тут, я вижив, мене не турбує ні майбутнє, ні гроші. Університет не виплатив відпускні, перевів на півставки, не дав зарплатні за піввересня, відправив на канікули за свій рахунок. Байдуже. Був спробував обуритися, довести себе до кондиції — нецікаво. Цікаво просто жити. Радію кицьці, що радісно муркоче до мене. Вона теж довгий час була в ступорі, не могла ні їсти, ні спілкуватися. Мені подобається ходити вулицями, бачити людей. Моя донька дорослішає, пофарбувала волосся, коротко підстриглася. Схожа на Алісу з «Гості з майбутнього» («Алісо, у майбутньому весело?» — «Та просто ахуїти».) Приємно думати, що я дожив. Їй подобається школа, уроки, але вона в цьому не зізнається. Чую, як відповідає в сусідній кімнаті, бачу, як готується до уроків. Українською їй задали написати легенду.

«Одного разу на місто і державу, в якій воно знаходиться, напала сусідня країна. Вона пускала ракети, стріляла з танків, бомбила літаками. І всі діти цього міста змушені були спуститися в підвали та льохи. Вони сиділи тиждень, два, три, місяць та більше. Без сонця та вуличних ігор ставали сумнішими і сумнішими і ні з ким не хотіли спілкуватися. Ані з батьками, ані з друзями. Але кожна дитина мала по кішці. Пухнасті, м'які, вони муркотіли дітям, заспокоювали їх. Діти розмовляли лише з кішками. Коли війна закінчилася і діти вийшли з льохів, виявилося, що кожна дитина мала по кішці, яка врятувала її. Про це дізналися всі городяни і поставили кішкам пам'ятник і по всьому місту миски, в які щоранку наливали молоко. З того часу традиція збереглася і кішок усі поважають».[9]

Кицька кусає мені руку, запрошує до гри. Я приймаю запрошення.

Translated by Andriy Lysenko

---

9 В оригіналі легенда дається українською.

J'écris avec des mots

Gassia Artin

En traversant des frontières,
Sans aucun droit,
Sans papier,
Hors la loi,
En effraction,
J'entre dans des lexiques étrangers
Je vole leurs mots et leurs verbes . . .
Au masculin, au féminin,
Au présent et au passé.

Je vole, et
Je cours avec.
Des pavés de mots et de lettres.
Entre deux parenthèses enchantées
Je construis des phrases et des pensées
Je transcris, bien appliquée,
Des expressions, des jeux de mots.
Volés à une langue étrangère.

Je vole des mots . . .
Tes mots . . .
Des mots entendus dans la rue Des mots attrapés en plein vol
Lors de rencontres étranges, étrangères.
Dans des pays, ici, ailleurs
Dans des avions, dans les nuages . . .

Capturés par mes pensées,
Inscrits, brodés,
Crochetés, fantasmés . . .
Détournés avec malice,
Des bonheurs et des tristesses.

Personne ne pourra plus les voler.
Je me les approprie et je les fais miens.
Je m'approprie ta langue
Etrangère.

Paris, 21 octobre 2018

Пишу словами

Гасся Артен

Без жодного посвідчення особи,
Й найменшої поваги до законів
Я проникаю за усі кордони,
Щоб викрасти з чужого лексикону
Слова, слова, слова
У всіх часах,
Родах, відмінках й видах дієслова.

А щойно викраду,
Мерщій тікати з ними
Опуклою бруківкою шрифтів;
Магічних дужок кола
Проривою
Закляттями
Які створила з
Незвичних виразів і чужослівних ігор.

Краду слова
Твої і перехожих,
У потягах, країнах і з ефіру,
У літаках, ба навіть у небес . . .

А всі оці присвоєні скарби
Одразу віддаю на переплавку;
Вплітаю щільно

У свої думки,
І власними чуттями прошиваю.

Нікому не дано
Забрати їх,
Вони-бо стали не моїми — мною!
Роблю своєю раз почуту мову:
Чи ж розпізнаєш тут слова свої?

Париж, 21 жовтня 2018
Translated by Andriy Lysenko

I Write with Words

Gassia Artin

Crossing borders
Without any right to
Undocumented
Irregular
I break and enter
Foreign vocabularies
I steal their nouns and verbs . . .
In all genders
Past and present.

I steal the words
And run away
Slabs of word and letter
Between enchanted parentheses
I make sentences and thoughts
Diligently transcribe
Wordplay, and say
Stolen in another way.

I steal words . . .
Your words . . .
Words overheard on the street, words on the wing
During strange meetings with strangers
In foreign lands, here, there
In airplanes, in the clouds . . .

Caught up in my thoughts
Inscribed, stitched
Knit together, fantasized . . .
Angrily pushed away,
Joys and sorrows.

No one can steal them back
I take your words and make them
Mine. My language, not a
Stranger's.

Paris, October 21, 2018
Translated by Alisa Slaughter

Ukraine—A Polyphony

ariel rosé

I meet a guy on a train (someday I will write a saga about the people I've met on trains). I ask him if the seat next to him is free. He is unable to answer. Finally he mumbles something incomprehensible in English. "Are you from Finland?" I ask. "How did you know?" "From your accent, I lived in Finland for a bit."

Tomi is returning from Kharkiv. Earlier he'd been in Severodonetsk, and earlier still near Kyiv. Immediately after the war broke out, he had volunteered with the French Foreign Legion. He had fought with them earlier as well, after the invasion of Crimea.

"What's Kharkiv like now?" I ask because my friend's son is there. "Not good, it's shelled. Do you know about the Wagner group?" I nod. I am worrying about Natalia's son who cannot leave Kharkiv. "What about Severodonetsk?" Tomi says he has a video clip from there. He gets his iPhone and shows me footage shot by one of his friends, with soldiers moving among the ruins of houses and shooting. The Russian soldiers are so close that you can hear their responses to a legionnaire shouting "Fuck you!" at them. I look into his unbelievably blue eyes, "Did anyone close to you die?" "Yes. A friend. You know, I don't want to fight at all. This war is horrible. It shouldn't be like this. I met someone from Caritas, and I am thinking about returning there as a Caritas volunteer."

I look at his lizard-like tattoos and wonder how he copes with all of this when falling asleep at night, if he sleeps at all. But Tomi is a Finn, and Finns believe in magic. He is on his way to Karelia to meet with his witch. She will heal him by drumming and singing. She cannot bleed him because his entire body is covered with scars. After that he will move on to his home in Rovaniemi where his eleven-year-old daughter lives. I see her face and her long fair hair on a photo in his phone.

Tomi has not had a drink for eleven years. Not one. He doesn't smoke. "I have only one weakness," he admits, and I am a little scared. "It's chocolate," he says, and his eyes smile. "In the army they said that I'm a bit like a woman, so delicate that all I can eat is chocolate."

"Do you have an ideal place that you would like to live—anywhere in the world?" he asks me suddenly. "There are no perfect places in the world. I need a little civilization and a little nature, ideally. What about you?" I see he really wants to tell me about his place. "Africa." He went there to fight. He loves the people, it's all about people. Especially the Eritreans and the Kenyans. Wonderful people. He also was in New Caledonia because the French Legion sent him there to learn French. I think to myself that there must be no better place to learn French. It is as if he is reading my thoughts. "It is a strange place, the islands are strange." He learned a slightly different French than the Parisian one. Perhaps more refined . . .

I wonder if this witch in Karelia will be enough for him. Doesn't he need therapy? Yes, he has had therapy. And he writes poetry. He pulls out his phone and lets me read. A death metal band wrote some music to his lyrics.

I see that Tomi is tired. We exchange wishes for the end of this war. He pulls his hat over his eyes. I leave him like that when I change to my Berlin train.

The Language of Tenderness

From my Berlin apartment I can see a chestnut tree outside my window; it drops its fruit and its leaves are being slowly eaten by time clothed in brown. In the corner store I spot Gorbachev vodka, filtered four times, and crystal clear, of course. Mikhail Gorbachev died a few days ago. It was because of him that the regime collapsed, even if he tried to save it by supplying some oxygen in the form of glasnost and perestroika. Nonetheless, that same Gorbachev supposedly said, "The Soviet Union without Ukraine is unconceivable" (*Ukrainian Weekly*, November 24, 1991). The Soviet Union appeared to some as an iceberg, after the melting of which entities appeared that previously seemed not to exist, such as the Baltic countries and Ukraine. In 1989, the "Law on Language" was adopted, which recognized Ukrainian as the only official language of the country. Before that, a diglossia existed: there was a division into a superior language, that is, Russian, and an inferior language, that is, Ukrainian. “The 1980s were a national rebirth,” Yurii Andrukhovych (age sixty-three) tells me over Zoom from his Ivano-Frankivsk apartment where the air raid siren no longer sounds as often as it did. “Language was the number one topic. The law on the language caused a big debate in the society.” Yurii became active in rescuing the language as if it were an endangered species. It was necessary to create special conditions for it, new publications, and take care of the ecology of culture and the ecology of spirit. Perhaps a nation is an imagined community, as Benedict Anderson put it, yet it is difficult to regard languages as imagined entities.

In Berlin not a day passes without me hearing either Russian, Polish, or Turkish. Spring is in full bloom when I meet Daryna Gladun (age thirty-one) on Viktoria-Luise-Platz across from the Potemkin Restaurant. This makes me feel uneasy and I promise myself never to visit this place. Daryna is dressed all in black and wears a fanny pack across her chest like a sash. She suggests going to Alexanderplatz (named after Russian Tsar Alexander I) to an exhibition of Ukrainian artists. We walk through the exhibit in the basement of a former distillery wearing masks (it's still Covid) and looking at the evidence of Russian crimes. Daryna tells me about them in a calm voice, like in a meditation session, as if she wanted to detach herself from what we are looking at. She escaped Bucha at the very last moment.

There was no transportation anymore, and she and Lesyk Panasiuk had to walk for several kilometers. After we leave the basement I ask her how I can help her now. Does she need someone to talk to, or be silent with? No, she has already developed her ritual: she goes to the Dussmann bookstore and finds calm among the mass of books. But I can't find calm. I start to run. I can't stop and end up running all the way home across half of Berlin. The same day Lesyk Panasiuk sends me pictures of their apartment in Bucha, to which he has returned to install new windows. Scattered shards of glass from the window panes litter the floor. They cover books and everything else like frozen snow.

I remember this a few months later when I am sitting in the Potemkin restaurant. (I won't ever tell this to anyone. I won't try to explain how I was caught by a big rainstorm at Viktoria-Luise-Platz and went there for shelter.) I hear Russian all around me, and I feel uneasy as the rain grows heavier. I just returned from Paris where Indian summer was at its peak. There I sat in a Paris apartment together with Ella Yevtushenko (age twenty-six) and Anna Malihon (age forty) after a launching an event for an anthology of Ukrainian poetry published by Maison de la Poésie. Two days earlier Ella was in Nancy at a hotel restaurant, when an app on her cellphone sounded an air raid alarm. Inside the luxurious hotel, the publisher, the members of the Académie Goncourt—they all froze. Ella had forgotten to turn off the app upon leaving Kyiv. Red-haired and wearing a green flowered dress, Ella, who looks like an elf, tells me that Russian was spoken at her home because her mother was Russian. Ukrainian was Ella's conscious choice, even if initially it was like a foreign tongue, "I had to translate everything in my head." Still, she would read world literature in Russian, as the Ukrainian translations did not satisfy her. She calls the Russian language a colonial heritage. "To speak is to exist absolutely for the other," wrote Frantz Fanon, who comes from Martinique. The colonizers, by depriving their subjects of language, *de facto* deprived them of the ability for true expression or linguistic habits, as Sartre put it, likely taken from Edward Sapir. "How could they, after so many years, renounce French," wonders Isabelle Macor, the French translator of my Polish poetry, as we dine together. Sartre maintained that, while trying to assimilate to the colonizer's culture, one abandons one's own identity. "Everything had to be perceived through Russian lenses," Natalia Trokhym tells me over the phone from sweltering Kutaisi in Georgia while picking grapes that grow on the wall of her house, "Everything was about giving in to the Russian culture. Now it's the time to recognize ourselves."

Sitting in a black sweatshirt in Lviv in front of his computer, Ostap Slivinsky tells me something similar, "It is not that the language is innocent. It is not just a tool for communication, but also of violence. In an occupied territory the signs are changed." He cannot imagine a return of Russian to Ukraine, or Russian literature. He says that a quarantine is needed. Only then did I realize that for him now Russian is like Covid.

"Language was the means of spiritual subjugation," wrote Ngugi wa Thiong'o. The Kenyan author abandoned English for the Kikuyu and Swahili languages. I am talking about this with Clara Simpson, an Irish actress living in Paris. "You know," Clara says, shaking her mop of blonde hair, "I wouldn't claim that the English language is not aggressive towards Irish." She remembers almost nothing of Irish. In the Introduction to his *Imagined Communities,* Benedict Anderson asked about national identities in their relations to countries, "Anyone who has doubts about the UK's claims to such parity with the USSR should ask himself what nationality its name denotes: Great Brito-Irish?"

On my way home I receive a message from Basel from Natalia Blok (age forty). Her paternal grandmother taught her in Russian. Natalia did not understand what her other grandmother and her mother were talking about in Ukrainian until she was five. I met Natalia many years ago during a residency in Gotland. She did not speak English then. I was the only person she could talk to in Russian, in my broken Russian. I never studied that language, but my mother read aloud to me poems by Mandelstam, Akhmatova, and Tsvetaeva in their original language. And LPs with songs by Okudzhava and Vysotsky were played around the clock. Even now I find that I sometimes unintentionally use words that are not Polish. A few months ago I asked a friend to help me carry my heavy *chemodan* down the stairs. He looked at me dumbfounded. So *chemodan* is not a Polish word . . . I did not know it was Russian. It originally came from the Persian. The BBC aired a program *Chamedan* on Iranian refugees. Polish *walizka,* on the other hand, comes from the French.

Upon returning to Berlin I learn that, starting tomorrow, Olga Bragina (age forty-one) has no place to stay. Her residency is ending. I invite her with her mother to stay at my place. Irina Krasnoper, a Russian poet who has lived in Berlin for many years, brings them over by car. Olga wears a flowered coat and her white shoes sparkle with little silver sequins. She tells me that a language is not owned by any single state. "Russian is not the property of the Russian Federation," declares

Olga. I speak Russian with her mother, to which Iya Kiva shakes her head when I tell her about it later over Zoom. To Iya, Russian is a room she does not want to enter. Russian was spoken in her home. She wrote poems in both languages, but now she consciously choses Ukrainian. "Russia and Ukraine are like a toxic relationship, and one constantly thinks about your ex instead of looking for someone new."

After the conversation with Iya I run to a reading by Ilya Kaminsky. He is participating in a literary festival in Berlin. After the reading we go for a walk. He tells me about his relative who, already after World War II, was shot on an Odesa street for speaking Yiddish. Ilya's poems are signed in sign language that I do not understand but observe with fascination. In the United States, from the end of the nineteenth century to the 1960s, deaf students were beaten and forced to sit on their palms so that they wouldn't use American Sign Language.

I recall the story of Natalia Trokhym from her kindergarten where children were compelled to speak Russian. She rebelled and, for speaking Ukrainian, was forced to stay out on a balcony in December with no warm clothing. She stood there like a statue. "It was my war, I wanted to win it, so I didn't cry." She got nephritis, and never returned to that kindergarten. It would be fair to say she won. Yuri Andruchovych's kindergarten used Soviet methods; the kids were told to speak Russian, and everybody addressed each other by their last names. Once, when picking Yuri up, his grandmother remarked, "All of you have Ukrainian names, why are you addressing each other in Russian?"

I leave for a few days: Paris, Stockholm, Bergen. I read poetry. I meet people from many countries. At a dinner after the Bergen festival Sonia tells me where she is from. From Portugal. So I ask if her native tongue is Portuguese. "It is complicated," she answers and changes the topic. But I am curious about the complicated. "You see, my father comes from Cabo Verde, he spoke Crioulo. Portuguese is the colonizer's language." Later he moved to Portugal where he met Sonia's mother, and they emigrated to Holland. Dutch is her *mother* tongue, she says. She went to Portugal once, but her grandparents laughed that she spoke Portuguese like a child.

I think about this at the Bergen airport while waiting for boarding when a message from Boris Khersonsky arrives. He is waiting for a train in Ravenna. He and Ludmila are at a residency in Italy. They were reluctant to leave Odesa. I remember the picture of their window blocked off with books in case of an explosion—a new use for books. At his home, "Odesa Russian" was spoken—a smoothie made of Yiddish, Russian, Polish, Ukrainian, with Bulgarian thrown somewhere in the middle. His parents sent him to a Russian school, but from second grade they insisted that he learn Ukrainian. He wrote in "Odesa Russian." "My Russian teacher liked my poems, and my Ukrainian teacher did not like my poems." However, these teachers had something in common—they were not good teachers. Marianna Kiyanovska tells me, "Boris made a significant decision, and after the Maidan he only writes in Ukrainian." "But I do not renounce Russian," he writes to me.

Marianna translated Boris's poems into Ukrainian. To do that, she had to find a new language. "Odesa Ukrainian" has a different syntax and a different phonetics. She had to create a language for that translation. I meet Marianna near the Grimm Zentrum library in Berlin. She wears a fabric necklace with a flowered folk design. At her home, only Ukrainian was spoken. Her grandfather did not keep books by Russian authors, except for Blok. Marianna knows Russian literature back and forth. Or, rather, from the inside, and as if from above. Chekhov and Gogol are not entirely Russian anymore. They are above this. Just like Conrad who was a little bit Polish and a little bit Ukrainian, yet he chose Africa to tell us about his legacy. This is not about Russian but about some higher language. Marianna translates from a high language, she tells me. It is not a propaganda language, or the language of political idiom, as this is a dead tongue. It is about a language where the *cogito* lives. Maybe it was not an accident that Marianna bought an apartment in Lviv not far from the place where Zbigniew Herbert had lived. He is one of a few Polish authors she did not translate for a long time because, as she says, she does not know how to translate irony. On the other hand, she can render a melody exquisitely, which I experience when she reads aloud her translation of Julian Tuwim's *Locomotive*, and I feel as if it is in Polish. It is as if she really found this metaphysical tongue above all divisions, as Walter Benjamin put it. Above the private tongue described by Wittgenstein.

At the end of the day I walk in the Tiergarten together with my biologist friends Olivia Judson and Alexandre Courtiol who want to show me beavers. Their sex organs are not visible, says Alexandre. You can't tell a male from a female by site, only by smell. Olivia is good at this. She can tell. We stand at the edge of the water sniffing. I only smell water. It is good. Olivia could tell that a pair of beavers had been there. We're too late. Or too early. It's hard to know, perhaps Hegel would.

About whom I talk to a German writer. "And here you go, *Hegel and Haiti,* she said, there is this book on the Haitian Revolution. About master and slave." And I think about Joseph Losey's film *The Servant,* based on Harold Pinter's play, about a servant who was in fact a master. And I think how Foucault wrote about this problem, and about biopolitics. Which brings me back to my biologist friends and our discussion on heritage, on how blood relations are about power. Genetics and blood are only biopolitics. I prefer feelings. And tenderness. Expressed in any language.

Translated by Frank L. Vigoda
Illustrated by ariel rosé

Two Poems

Ія Ківа

я хотіла б тобі сказати, що земля тут анітрошечки не змінилася,
але це буде неправда, це буде жорстока даремна брехня,
якою притрушують цупку дитячу цікавість

дерева тут лише удають дерева, дерева тут не вдаються,
піднімаючи гілля угору, немовби здаються в полон
своїм і чужим, і цьому сучому часу,
де з пуп'янків відразу ж народжуються сірники

а річка життя так добре горить, палає від сорому,
що пересохла, що не здатна більше наповнити
літо — джмелиним сміхом, а зиму — медом турботи

земля тут за рік так постаріла,
що там, де століттями бачили гладке личко води
тепер самі зморшки завглибшки з долоню,
а буває і гірше, так, наче сонце
світить тепер вниз головою, але хто тепер дивиться вгору

небо тут таке тихе, що кинь у нього ножем — не ворухнеться,
стерпить і це, ковтаючи мовчки кинджал за кинджалом,
роздираючи щоки до крові, як розривають на шмати одежу
що більше не захищає; око лихе, знаєш,

обмацує тебе зсередини, мов хтиві руки у натовпі,
спокійно, без сорому, з відчуттям повільного злочину,
аж до самого серця; і те зупиняється, а ти живеш далі;
але тихо, без серця; без сподівань; як пощастить

ось і земля тут тепер без серця, наче ґрунт у музеї,
лежить у всіх на очах напівжива, непритомна,
бо не встигнеш й повітря ковтнути, а воно вже отруєне —
дряпається, гарчить, ніби конає старенький собака

і так все це, знаєш, вигадливо, що всі вже навчилася
робити вигляд, наче не чують власного ж розкладання,
а смердить тепер так, що тільки за смородом своїх і впізнаєш —
таких гордих, таких принишклих, таких безжально красивих

смерть, знаєш, завжди додає краси; аж до судомного реготу;
хіба ж це не смішно — все життя ходити тією самою стежкою
і розминутись з собою на першому ж перехресті

хіба так буває; хіба цій землі не набридло
водити по колу з пов'язкою на очах, мов у грі в панаса;
гей, ти, нумо вгадай, де впадеш і не підведешся

стільки тут добрих людей, знаєш, а всі лежать у багнюці;
покотом; розкинувши руки; без голів, як прийдеться

ця земля — наче шрам на обличчі; бачать усі,
але спитати, що ж врешті сталося, бракує відваги;
життя, знаєш, занадто коротке, щоб вдивлятися в землю,
особливо в чужу; щось в цьому є від перелюбу

так, ніби любов раптом стала штучною мовою,
яку ми вчимо, і вчимо, і вчимо — тільки без сенсу

я хотіла тобі сказати, що земля ця — поезія
ти ж знаєш не гірше за мене скільки в поезії читачів

04–06 липня 2023

***

раз полишивши дім — не зупинитись в дорозі
не сказати ніколи вже: кидайте речі, ось, ми прийшли
адже кроки — єдина колиска яку, ти носиш на спині
не маючи права упасти, спинитись, зробити коло,
дихання мертвих дерев переспівати тремтінням зап'ястків

раз полишивши дім — не сховатись більше від цегли
між пальців, з якої будуєш гирло печалі,
печатку її накладаючи на фарбу і віск
часу, що лущиться, наче горіх з чорним серцем,
і під шкіру в'їдається як сонця шершавий язик

раз полишивши дім — не відшукати слів для любові
до місця, в якому впадеш у дитинства глухий коридор,
де речі ще виглядають тебе до гри, яка тоне під кригою щастя,
яке потемніло давно, мов бабусин перстень на пальці,
і стало важким, як родинний альбом на цвинтарі пам'яті

раз полишивши дім — не зазирнути вже у вікно,
за яким на тебе чекають розквітлі троянди життя,
бо твій сад відпливає разом з тобою, і вода,
чуєш, вода забирає в обійми тіло твоє,
сповнене спрагою моря, що, як свободу, не перейти

31 березня 2023

***

Iya Kiva

I'd like to tell you that the land here has not changed one bit,
but that would be untrue, the kind of cruel and futile lie
that they sprinkle to soothe a child's eager curiosity

the trees here only pretend to be trees, the trees here fail,
lifting up their branches, as if yielding themselves prisoners
in surrender to their own tribe, to strangers and to this bitch of an era
where matches are born straight from the buds

and the river of life burns so well, burning with shame,
that it has dried up, unable anymore to fill the summer
with bumblebee laughter and the winter with the honey of care

the land here has aged so much in one year
that where for centuries we saw the smooth pretty face of water
now the wrinkles are palm-deep
and it sometimes gets even worse, yes, as if the sun now
were shining upside down, but who looks up these days anyway

the sky here is so quiet, throw a knife at it and it won't flinch,
it'll endure this too, silently swallowing dagger after dagger,
tearing its cheeks to blood, as they tear to shreds clothes
that no longer protect; evil eye, you know,

it gropes you from within, like lusty hands in a crowd,
calmly, shamelessly, with the feel of unhurried crime,
to the very heart; and the heart stops while you live on;
but quietly, without a heart; without hope; at luck's mercy

and so, the land here, heartless now, like soil in a museum,
lies half alive and unconscious before everyone's eyes,
you barely have time to take in a gulp of air and it's already poisoned—
scratching, growling, like an old dog that is dying

and all of this is so, you know, fanciful, that everyone has learned
to pretend as that they can't smell their own decomposition,
it stinks so badly now that you only recognize your own by their stench—
those so proud, so subdued, so mercilessly beautiful

death, you know, always adds beauty; even to the point of convulsive laughter;
isn't it funny to walk the same path all your life
only to miss oneself at the very first intersection

how could this be real; isn't this earth sick of going around
in circles in with blindfolded eyes, as in a game of blind man's buff;
hey, you, come on, guess where you'll fall and not get up

so many good people here, you know, and they all lie in the mire;
in heaps; arms spread; headless, as the case may be

this land is like a facial scar; everyone sees it,
but the courage is lacking to ask what has actually happened;
life is too short, you know, to gaze pointblank at a land,
especially someone else's; there's a kind of adultery to it

as if love had suddenly become an artificial language
that we study and study it endlessly—only without meaning

I wanted to tell you that this land is poetry
and you know no worse than I how many readers poetry has

July 6, 2023

***

once you've left your home, you can never stop on the road
never say again: put down your baggage, we have arrived,
because footsteps are the only cradle you carry on your back
without the right to fall, to pause, to circle back
to sing with trembling wrists echoing the tremors of dead trees

once you've left your home, never hide between fingers
from the bricks from which you build up the throat of sorrow
pressing its seal onto the paint and wax
of time, which crumbles like a nut with a black heart
embedding itself under the skin like the sun's scratchy tongue

once you've left your home, words cannot be found for the love
of a place where you'll relapse into the silent corridor of childhood
where things eye you before a game that sinks through the ice of bliss
that darkened long ago, like grandmother's ring on your finger,
and grew as heavy as a family album in the memory cemetery

once you've left your home, you can't gaze into the window anymore
behind which the roses of a life in full bloom await you
because your garden has drifted away with you and water
can you hear, water is enveloping your body
filled with the thirst of a sea that, like freedom, is impossible to cross

March 31, 2023
Translated by Philip Nikolayev

***

Ija Kiwa

Chciałabym ci powiedzieć, że ziemia tutaj ani trochę się nie zmieniła,
ale to nie byłaby prawda, byłaby to okrutna, czcza brednia,
która tłumi dziecka ciekawość

Drzewa tutaj tylko udają drzewa, drzewa tutaj zawodzą,
podnoszą gałęzie w górę, jakby się poddając
swoim i obcym, i temu nieszczęsnemu czasowi,
gdzie z pąków w moment rodzą się zapałki

a rzeka życia tak dobrze płonie, płonie wstydem,
rzeka, która wyschła, której nie da się napełnić
śmiechem trzmieli — latem, kojącym miodem — zimą

ziemia się tak postarzała tutaj w ciągu roku
gdzie od stuleci widzieliśmy gładką twarz wody
tam pojawiły się zmarszczki na głębokość dłoni
a bywa i gorzej, tak, gdy słońce
świeci do góry nogami, ale kto by dzisiaj patrzył w górę

niebo tu takie ciche, rzuć w nie nożem — ani się poruszy
zniesie i to, łykając sztylet za sztyletem,
rozdzierający policzki do krwi, jak rozdziera się płaszcz na strzępy,
który już nie chroni; złe oko, wiesz,

obmacuje cię od środka, jak lubieżne ręce w tłumie,
spokojnie, bez wstydu, z poczuciem powolnej zbrodni,
aż do samego serca, które zamiera, gdy ty żyjesz dalej,
tylko po cichu, bez serca; bez nadziei, jak los chce

oto i ziemia teraz bez serca, jak ziemia w muzeum,
leży na oczach wszystkich, półżywa, nieprzytomna,
ani zdążysz złapać powietrza, już jest zatrute —
drapie, warczy, jak konający, stary pies

i wszystko takie, wiesz, niezwykłe, co już wszyscy pojęli,
jak udawać, że nie słyszą własnego rozkładu,
a teraz śmierdzi tak, że tylko po smrodzie innych swój poznajesz —
tych dumnych, stłumionych, bezlitośnie pięknych

śmierć, wiesz, zawsze dodaje piękna, aż do konwulsyjnego śmiechu;
czy to nie zabawne — chodzić całe życie tą samą ścieżką?
i rozminąć się na pierwszym skrzyżowaniu?

pewnie tak bywa; pewnie ziemia ma już dość
krążyć tak na ślepo, jakby grano z nią w ciuciubabkę;
hej, ty, zgaduj, gdzie upadniesz i już nie wstaniesz

jest tylu dobrych ludzi, wiesz, a wszyscy leżą w błocie;
pokotem; z rozrzuconymi rękami, bez głów, jak przystało

ziemia ta — niczym blizna na twarzy, którą wszyscy widzą,
ale brak odwagi zapytać, co właściwie się stało;
wiesz, życie za krótkie, by wpatrywać się w ziemię,
szczególnie w cudzą, jest w tym coś z cudzołóstwa

tak, jakby miłość zamieniła się nagle w sztuczny język,
którego się ciągle uczymy i uczymy — tylko pozbawiony jest sensu

chciałam ci powiedzieć, że ta ziemia to poezja
i wiesz nie gorzej niż ja, ilu poezja ma czytelników

06 lipca 2023

***

Opuściwszy dom — nie zatrzymuj się w drodze
nigdy nie mów nigdy; odłóż rzeczy, oto jesteśmy
kroki przecież to jedyna kołyska, jaką nosisz na plecach
bez prawa do upadku, do przestanku, by zatoczyć koło,
oddech martwych drzew śpiewał wraz z drżeniem nadgarstków

opuściwszy dom, nie ukryjesz dłużej cegły
między palcami, z której budujesz usta smutku
odciskając jej piętno na farbie i wosku
czasu, co zdejmuje łupinę, jak orzecz z czarnym sercem,
i wdziera się pod skórę niczym słońca szorstki język

opuściwszy dom — nie znajdujesz słów na miłość
tam, gdzie wpadasz w głuchy korytarz dzieciństwa,
gdzie czekają na ciebie rzeczy do gry, które toną pod lodem szczęścia,
które już dawno pociemniało, jak pierścionek babci na palcu
i stało się ciężkie niczym album rodzinny na cmentarzu pamięci

opściwszy dom — nie patrz przez okno,
za którym czekają na ciebie kwitnące róże życia,
bo wraz z tobą unosi się twój ogród, a woda,
czujesz, woda bierze twoje ciało w ramiona,
spragniona morza, którego jak wolności, nie można przekroczyć

31 marca 2023
Translated by ariel rosé

The Invincible Nightingale: Ukrainian Poetry as an Antidote to War[1]

Svetlana Lavochkina

The shape of Ukraine on the geographical map resembles a bird with a human head, its delicate, spirited profile lifted up. In Slavic mythology, this mythical creature possessed demiurgic powers: having hatched out of celestial oak acorns, it dived into the depths of the sea, reached solid ground and heaved it onto the Earth's surface. On the map, this Bird of Ukraine looks as if it were taking a brief repose after its labors, its wings folded, its two feet, the Crimea and the Odesa Region, dipped in the Black Sea, its rump snugly ensconced on the Sea of Azov. Its feathers are thick rustling forests, or fecund steppes, wild and field-tamed. Its blue river arteries, its countless rivulet veins nourish vigorous cities and serene hamlets. Ukraine's sanguine heart pulses with theaters, concert halls, universities, bookshops. Skyscrapers and huts alike sparkle with their window-eyes, and the cooking stoves from Luhansk in the east to Lviv in the west conjure up redolent meals. And each cell of the Bird of Ukraine is imbued with its spiritual DNA—the agile, melodious, and colorful language, famed for its polyphonic complexity, as if custom-made for composing poetry. Indeed, Ukrainians call their language "our nightingale tongue." In Ukrainian poems, trumpets and fanfares of turbulent

---

1 First commissioned for "Paper Sanctuary: Pragmatism & Poetry for Ukrainian Refugees," the Humanitarian Pavilion for London Design Biennale 2023, by Japanese architect Shigeru Ban in collaboration with Svetlana Lavochkina, photographer Vincent Haiges, and composer Valentin Silvestrov, curated by Clare Farrow Studio.

history resound, violins and lutes sing of love, tambourines sparkle with humor and wit, and even the cello of sadness pours mellow.

The shape of Ukraine on the map faces west: a valiant country that, in 1991, chose to turn its back on the Soviet past and live as an independent European democracy. Yet, for centuries, our nightingale has been dwelling under an overcast sky. Russia, a predator hawk-state to its north and east, has always deemed Ukraine game to be devoured. Since 2014, the nightingale's Crimea foot has been trapped, and its rump, Donbas, has been singed. Since February 24, 2022, the whole body of Ukraine is one raw wound, plucked, bleeding, lead-shot. But the nightingale lives nonetheless, undefeated, defiant, and free. Out of the black seas of the psyche, it is heaving courage and indomitable spirit to resist.

Each and every Ukrainian is now a fighter for freedom, be it a soldier on the battlefield, a truck driver carrying relief supplies, a teacher in a half-ruined school, a waiter in a front zone café, a refugee mother crossing the border on foot, her baby in a sling.

Each and every Ukrainian is now the bard of resilience. Poetry has become an antidote to the poison of war, an antibiotic to festering wounds. It is a meticulous record of shellings and blackouts, war crimes, lost homes, and flight into the unknown. The tune is rendered monochrome, like the color of children's irises in bomb shelters. Chromatic opulence of colors can be neither perceived nor afforded in this night of war. Yet, as is the law of creation, as is the law of history, dawn will come, and justice will be restored. When the war wounds are healed in the sunshine of victory, colors will return in new splendor. The Ukrainian Nightingale will resume its flight in the shelling-free, cleansed blue skies, its spirited human profile faced westwards.

Непереможний соловейко: Українська поезія як протиотрута від війни[2]

Світлана Лавочкіна

Обриси України на мапі нагадують птаха з тонким, одухотвореним профілем задертої вгору людської голови. Слов'янська міфології наділяла цю міфічну істоту силами деміурга: щойно вона вилупилась з жолудя небесного дуба, як пірнула в морські глибини, досягла твердої землі і підняла її на поверхню. На мапі цей Птах-Україна виглядає так, ніби відпочиває після трудів: крила зведені, дві ноги — Крим і Одещина — занурені в Чорне море, а черевце затишно вмостилося на Азовському морі. Його пір'я — густі шелесткі ліси або родючі степи, дикі і оброблені. Її незліченні блакитні артерії і вени річок живлять метушливі міста і неквапні села. У її пульсуючому серці — театри, концертні зали, університети, книгарні. Однаково виблискують очима-вікнами хмарочоси і сільські хати, від Луганська на сході до Львова на заході чарують апетитними стравами кухні. І кожна клітинка Птаха-України просякнута її духовною ДНК — гнучкою, мелодійною, барвистою, ніби спеціально створеною для творення поезії мовою, що славиться своєю поліфонічною складністю. Українці називають свою мову «солов'їна». В українських віршах

---

2 Вперше представлено на виставці Гуманітарного павільйону Лондонської бієнале дизайну 2023 «Паперове святилище: прагматизм і поезія для українських біженців»: архітектор Шіґеру Бан (Японія) у співпраці зі Світланою Лавочкіною, фотографом Вінсентом Хейґесом і композитором Валентином Сильвестровим, куратор — Clare Farrow Studio.

сурми і фанфари бурхливої історії, скрипки і лютні кохання, бубни гумору і дотепності, і навіть віолончель смутку ллються напрочуд м'яко.

Профіль України на мапі звернений на захід: відважна країна, яка в 1991 році вирішила відвернутися від радянського минулого і розвиватись як незалежна європейська демократія. Та протягом століть наш соловейко жив під похмурим небом. З півночі та сходу нависає Росія — хижа держава-яструб, що завжди вважала Україну бажаною здобиччю. З 2014 року солов'їна лапка-Крим опинилася в пастці, а пір'я хвостика-Донбасу обгоріло. З 24 лютого 2022 року все тіло України — суцільна свіжа рана, відкрита, кривава, начинена свинцевим дробом. Та попри, все соловейко живий, непереможений, зухвалий і вільний. З Чорного моря своєї душі він черпає мужність і незламність.

Кожен українець зараз — борець за свободу: солдат на полі бою, водій вантажівки з гуманітарною допомогою, вчитель у напівзруйнованій школі, офіціант у прифронтовій кав'ярні, мати-біженка, яка пішки перетинає кордон з немовлям у слінгах.

Кожен українець зараз є бардом стійкості. Поезія стала антидотом до отрути війни, антибіотиком до гнійних ран. Це скрупульозний запис обстрілів і знеструмлень, воєнних злочинів, втрачених домівок і втеч у невідомість. Мелодія монохромна, як колір райдужок дитячих оченят у бомбосховищах. У ніч війни не до розмаїття кольорів. Та, врешті-решт, закони світоладу візьмуть своє: настане світанок і справедливість буде відновлено. Коли рани війни загояться під сонцем перемоги, кольори повернуться у новій красі. Український соловейко відновить свій політ в очищеному від ракет блакитному небі, а його одухотворений людський профіль усміхнеться.

Translated by Andriy Lysenko

Február huszonnégy

Marianna Gyurász

Hajnali öt volt, mikor arra ébredtem, hogy a
gyomorsavam lassan kúszik fel a mellkasomban,
és hiába nyúltam a bögre vízért,
valahogy az ötödik, a tizedik, a tizenötödik korty sem segített
lejjebb kényszeríteni a feltoluló éles, zsibbasztó szorongást,

pedig fogalmam sem volt
hányan ülnek most ugyanígy,

félig felhúzott térddel, értetlenül,
érthetetlenül hitetlenkedve azon,
hogy mégiscsak
törékeny, tűpontos, törékeny óraművek
vagyunk mind,

mindannyian visszaszámolunk.

February twenty-four

Marianna Gyurász

At five AM
I woke to the
sensation of
slow acid creeping up
my chest,
and I reached in vain for
the mug of water,
somehow the fifth,
tenth, the fifteenth sip
could not
force down the sharp,
numbing anxiety that
was rising,

though I had no idea
how many sat in
the same way,

with their knees half
drawn up,
uncomprehending,
in incomprehensible
disbelief,
that after all
we are all fragile, precise, fragile
clockworks
we all count down.

Translated by Gábor Danyi and Alisa Slaughter

Двадцять четверте лютого

Марианна Гюрас

Прокинулась о п'ятій на світанку,
у роті кисло і пече вогнем,
та марно я ковтаю воду з склянки,
таких пожеж не гасить H_2O.
й тривоги язики лише нещадніш.

а скільки ще таких же,
в тій же позі,

зіщулені, з руками на колінах,
людей як я у той же ж ранній час,
не вірячи новинам і очам,
на таймери у мент перетворились,

щоб як точніш дорахувати до . . .

Translated by Andriy Lysenko

On Sand and Silt

Alisa Slaughter

Late spring, 2023: the North Atlantic is hot, three or four degrees Celsius hotter than normal, and rescuers are searching for a small submarine. It contains explorers lost while looking around the wreck of the *Titanic*. The hot Atlantic and the lost submarine feel related, but they are not, of course, except at some profound level, a *benthic* connection, to borrow the scientific term.

In the Mediterranean, they aren't sure if they can ever recover the 600 or so people who drowned when a smuggling boat capsized last week, and, in the Black Sea, tons of pollutants are settling into estuaries after a massive manmade flood on the Dnipro River.

I. Sandy Biotopes

For so-called fun, I help out at a restoration project in a tiny sand dune habitat where two transverse mountain ranges meet in Southern California. Spanish colonial explorers gave the mountain ranges their names: the San Gabriels and the San Bernardinos. The river that still intermittently runs nearby, the Santa Ana, helped create the dunes and atmospherics where the Pacific, the Gulf of California, and the Sonoran and Colorado Deserts meet the mountains, the winds push fires in unpredictable directions, and the climate wobbles between damp and dry.

The work is straightforward: pull invasive mustard, collect trash, and set cedar shims to keep the sand from blowing away. Along with plastic toys, tires, and carpet scraps, we excavate old, futile attempts to stabilize the dunes: plastic mesh fencing, weed cloth, and now the shims, not made of plastic themselves though bundled in strips of it. All the effort serves an insect few of us will ever see, the endangered Delhi Sands flower-loving fly. This federally listed species prevents a few bits of the long alluvial plain from incorporation into the region's vast logistics hub. Surrounded by freeways, railroad tracks, million-square-foot warehouses, and landfills, the fly emerges every summer and feeds—they think—on the wire lettuces, buckwheats, and tarweeds its name suggests it loves.

II. Sandy Biotopes, Eastern Version

On June 6, 2023, the Russian military detonated explosives on the Kakhovka Dam, flooding the downstream regions of the Dnipro River. The human cost is enormous, and the environmental significance of this disaster, which Ukrainian scientists say is the most significant ecological effect on the region in the past 100 years, will occupy lifetimes of work for biologists. The landscape names echo their own historical and geographical specificity: Ponto-Sarmatic deciduous thickets, Euro-Siberian dwarf-annual amphibian swards, Lower Dnipro Sands. The river's human history and ancient geomorphology has created a complicated and biologically rich web of hydrology, soil types, and ecological co-dependencies. Such specialized habitats and species require years or decades to recover under the best circumstances; more violence, invasion, and exploitation will further devastate the area.[1]

III. Invasions Big and Small

The United States invaded Mexico—the last full-scale invasion, it might be termed—in 1847, and the treaty that followed created the US/Mexican/Native palimpsest where I and millions of other humans live, and where creatures like the Delhi Sands fly—and the Western burrowing owl, the Santa Ana sucker, and the California gnatcatcher struggle to survive. Since that time, the United States has intervened in Mexico on scales less than full: CIA interference in liberatory

---

1 For a detailed overview of the habitats, species, and general ecosystems affected by the disaster, see "The Consequences of the Russian Terrorist Attack on the Kakhovka Hydroelectric Power Plant (HPP) for Wildlife," UNCG, June 7, 2023, https://uncg.org.ua/en/the-consequences-of-the-russian-terrorist-attack-on-the-kakhovka-hydroelectric-power-station-hps-for-wildlife/.

movements in the 1960s and 1970s, the disastrous "war on drugs" that flooded the country with weapons and violence, and recent calls by right-wing politicians to "invade Mexico" as a response to irregular immigration.

Even outside declared states of crisis, filibuster armies of entrepreneurial Americans—pro-slavery expansionists or, later, veterans of the defeated Confederate military forces—penetrated as far south as Venezuela in a quest for colonial outposts. At the church in Caborca, Sonora, visitors can see bullet marks on the façade where locals fought off the *filibusteros*. They executed the surviving invaders except for one teenage boy.

Mexico has never been free of the threat of invasion or its colonial burden, at least in its recorded history. It shares a context with all of the Americas apart from the United States and Canada, who compounded the prosperity of their original colonizers. Along the border, the Tohono O'odham and Kumeyaay once adapted to this land, and now face the triple threat of climate change, border interdiction, and crime. Gangsters and hoodlums threaten their access to traditional food sources and motivate formal and informal states of exception where extortion, expropriation, and kidnapping are safer bets than drug smuggling for criminals, and law enforcement is almost as dangerous as the cartels. Venezuelan, Haitian, and Guatemalan refugees wait for a chance at asylum near fortified crossings—Mexicali, San Luis, Tijuana, Nogales—or risk their lives on the Rio Grande or the endless desert.

The border is a crooked line. Brownsville, Texas, and its twin city of Matamoros, Tamaulipas, sit at 25 degrees 90 minutes north by latitude, and San Diego, California, and its twin city of Tijuana, Baja California, at 32 degrees 71 minutes. It is easy to imagine the state of Texas looking like a tooth, part of a greedy mouth that bit a big chunk out of its neighbor to the south. The 100th meridian, which separates the humid east from the arid west, hits Mexico just a few hours northwest of Matamoros in the state of Nuevo Leon, near Laredo. Before agriculture and urban development tapped rivers and drove them underground, the Gila, the Rio Bravo, the Colorado River were once riparian highways that knitted the region together. Now, satellite photos show dry riverbeds and neat green circles and clean edges indicating irrigated agriculture and border installations. Crossing at official checkpoints is nearly impossible without documents, and, away from them, smugglers exploit desperate and vulnerable people. Hundreds have died unrecorded in the desert.

IV. Russia, Ukraine, and Post-Colonial Incoherence

Imperial Russia and its inheritors share their own histories of penal geography, entrepreneurial violence, and corruption. Along with its invasion of Ukraine, the Russian government's persecution of its own civil society—recently the Memorial organization, including the arrest and criminal prosecution of its co-founder—illustrates how it has at best not addressed its responsibility for internal and external colonialism. Much as a Latvian or a Chechen might have a great deal to discuss with a Puerto Rican or Chamorro resident of Guam, or a member of the Sami or Buryat people might find common ground with the Navajo and the Lakota, Ukrainians and Mexicans might find some commonalities in their histories of distinctive culture, strong identity, and imperiled sovereignty. That the Aztec Empire overlapped in time with the Zaporozhian Sich may or may not say much, but a Tohono O'odham farmer on a small holding in Sonora still shares the same awareness of soil and rainfall, melons and peppers with a Crimean Tatar on her bit of land; a shop owner in Hermosillo and one in Donetsk.

V. "No War"

One of the items confiscated from the Memorial organization's headquarters was a sticker with the motto "No War." The language of peace has become a twirling blade, accusing Russia one moment for its homicidal invasion, and accusing Ukraine's Western supporters as "warmongers" for supplying weapons the next. Political analysts point to the "non-aligned" discourse and canny active measures in support of anti-colonial and civil rights movements starting only a few years after the Russian Revolution. The discourse of racism, immigration, invasions both straightforward and metaphorical hits pockets of poison—or sentimentality, sweeter but just as toxic—as Ukrainian refugees flee for Europe and the Ukrainians legitimately demand unequivocal support. Everyone is asked to be an amateur geopolitical analyst: is the notion of a cross-border commons an irresoluble affront to sovereignty? Does an invasion lose its stink after a couple of hundred years, or is the mutilation permanent?[2]

---

2 See Sergio Gonzalez Rodriguez, *The Iguala 43* (Los Angeles: Semiotexte, 2017); and Sayak Valencia, *Gore Capitalism* (Los Angeles: *Semiotexte*, 2018), for extensive discussions of Latin

VI. If the Heat Doesn't Get You, the Humidity Will

The National Butterfly Center in Mission, Texas, is home to more than 60 species, including the lovely Mexican blue-wing. In the lower Rio Grande Valley, heat indexes regularly exceed 120 degrees Fahrenheit (49 degrees Celsius); in such a climate, a person can die of exposure in a few hours. In Mexicali, along the California/Baja border, the climate is drier but actual heat also reaches 120 degrees, and heat exhaustion regularly kills people in the Mexicali Valley—agricultural and construction workers, but also people who live outdoors because they are recently deported or waiting to cross the border, or suffer from the social ills associated with the drug trade. The land is lethal without infrastructure such as vehicles and air-conditioned buildings—or without centuries of adaptation—but running machines and clearing vegetation for development just makes it hotter, a frustrating paradox.[3]

When they filed suit against "We Build the Wall," a right-wing group that actually did build a private three-mile section of border wall—along with swindling donors out of many thousands of dollars—the hazards the Butterfly Center listed included possible damage to their own property and the Anzalduas dam downstream.[4] The structure is poorly engineered, but even the US Government's own wall needs constant monitoring to fight the natural effects of water and wind.

American and particularly Mexican approaches to questions of civil society, sovereignty, and responsibility.

3 There is significant documentation of the health and ecological effects of extreme heat, and the "urban heat island" phenomenon. See Polioptro Martinez-Austria and Erick R. Bandala, "Maximum Temperatures and Heat Waves in Mexicali, Mexico: Trends and Threshold Analysis," *Air, Soil and Water Research*, February 4, 2016; and Jeremy Hernandez-Rios et al., "Characterization of Patients with Guillain-Barré Syndrome in the General Hospital of Mexicali," *International Journal of Medical Students* 7, no. 3 (2019) for Mexicali-specific research. There is also an increasingly visible analysis of heat, inequality, and city design, see, for example, these recent articles: Damian Carrington, "Global Heating will Push Billions outside 'Human Climate Niche,'" *Guardian*, May 22, 2023, https://www.theguardian.com/environment/2023/may/22/global-heating-human-climate-niche; and Akshat Rathi, "Cities Must Be Redesigned for a Future of Extreme Heat," *Bloomberg*, May 18, 2023, https://www.bloomberg.com/news/articles/2023-05-18/cities-must-be-redesigned-for-a-future-of-extreme-heat.

4 See the page at the Butterfly Center's website, accessed October 9, 2024, https://www.nationalbutterflycenter.org/index.php?option=com_content&view=article&id=310&catid=9&Itemid=626, for details of the lawsuit and the Butterfly Center's response to a settlement that allows the three miles of wall to stand despite deep erosion scars in the Rio Grande riverbank that threaten its structural integrity.

The Butterfly Center's objections to the wall and to incursions onto their land by the Border Patrol and armed vigilantes made them a further target for threats and menacing behavior by right-wing extremists. The director wrote an anguished update after they reopened, lamenting that an organization dedicated to some of the prettiest and most delicate insects on earth needed to "harden" their site and train their staff to stop bleeding in case someone is attacked on their property.

VII. No Place is No Place

In spring of 2021, I visited Quitobaquito Spring, which the Tohono O'odham farmed—sustainably, to use that troubled adverb—for hundreds of years before the US government set up a national monument, now Organ Pipe National Park, and evicted the residents. A new, supposedly state-of-the-art section border wall runs within a few yards and already has piles of sediment and deep gashes where heavy rains dug gullies. The Sonoran Desert is a lively ecosystem where bighorn sheep, pronghorn antelope, the American jaguar, and countless smaller creatures need to move freely to find water, food, and shelter. When border infrastructure was a few obelisks and occasional barbed wire, it didn't do much damage, but new bright lights, coils of razor wire, excavation, and constant vehicle patrols now create a no-life zone for people and creatures. The Park Service is trying to figure out how to fix the damage to the spring, which now looks like a badly-built "water feature" on someone's ranchette, complete with ragged weed cloth and broken plastic piping. A few miles to the east, the State of Arizona improvised walls of shipping containers to perform the governor's political theater. The courts finally ordered them to take down the container wall and repair the damage.

At the Kakhovka Dam, scientists worry about the benthic life of the river, the multitudes of tiny creatures that form the basis of the food chain. It's poignant and horrifying to imagine their plight, trapped in the depths with no oxygen, without the things they need. They weren't fleeing a famine or drowned in their basements, or embarked on a risky excursion to explore someone else's bad idea, they are not sentient in the usual way, and so it is futile to imagine how they would suffocate as I would suffocate. Maybe it's too deep for me.

На піску і намулі

Аліса Слотер

Пізня весна 2023 року: у Північній Атлантиці спекотно: на три-чотири градуси за Цельсієм гарячіш, ніж зазвичай, рятувальники шукають маленьку субмарину з дослідниками, які зникли під час вивчення місця катастрофи «Титаніка». Гаряча Атлантика і зникла субмарина здаються пов'язаними, хоча, звичайно, це й не так, хіба що на якомусь глибинному, ба навіть бентичному рівні.

Не відомо, чи вдасться колись знайти 600 нелегалів, потонулих у Середземному морі під час кораблетрощі, що сталась тиждень тому, а після масштабної антропогенної повені на Дніпрі в Чорне море потрапили тони забруднюючих речовин.

I. Піщані біотопи

Заради так званої розваги я допомагаю у проекті з відновлення крихітного біотопу піщаних дюн у місці зустрічі двох поперечних гірських хребтів Південної Каліфорнії. Іспанські колоністи дали цим хребтам назви: Сан-Габріель і Сан-Бернардіно. Річка Санта-Ана, що вона, нехай з перебоями, але все ще протікає неподалік, сприяла утворенню дюн і атмосфери, де Тихий океан, Каліфорнійська затока й пустелі Соноран і Колорадо зустрічаються з горами, вітри розносять пожежі в непередбачуваних напрямках, а клімат коливається між вологим і сухим.

Робота проста: вириваємо інвазивну гірчицю, збираємо сміття та встановлюємо кедрові прокладки, щоб не вивітрювався пісок. Разом із пластиковими іграшками, шинами та клаптиками килимів ми викопуємо старі, марні засоби стабілізації дюн: огорожі з пластикової сітки, агротканину проти бур'янів і більш сучасні підкладки, що вони хоча й зроблені не з пластику, але перев'язані його смужками. Все це заради комахи, яку мало хто з нас колись побачить — зникаючої делійської піщаної мухи-квіткоїдки. Ця занесена до списку зникаючих видів комаха не дозволяє кільком ділянкам довжелезної алювіальної рівнини влитися до величезного логістичного хабу регіону. Затиснена автострадами, залізничними коліями, складами площею в мільйони квадратних футів і звалищами, муха з'являється щоліта і, згідно із відображеними у її назви вподобаннями, харчується нектаром квітів каліфорнійської гречки і латуку.

II. Піщані біотопи, східна версія

6 червня 2023 року російські військові підірвали Каховську дамбу, що спричинило затоплення регіонів, розташованих нижче за течією Дніпра. Людські жертви величезні, а нинішнім біологам доведеться присвятити все своє життя, аби тільки оцінити масштаби катастрофи, яку українські вчені називають найзначнішим екологічним впливом на регіон за останні 100 років. Назви ландшафтів перегукуються з їхньою історичною та географічною специфікою: Понтично-сарматські листопадні чагарники, Євро-сибірські низькорослі однорічні земноводні угруповання, Нижньодніпровські піски. Історія використання річки людиною та давня геоморфологія утворили складне і біологічно багате переплетення гідрології, типів ґрунтів та екологічних взаємозалежностей. Навіть за найкращих обставин такі спеціалізовані біотопи та види потребують років або й десятиліть для відновлення; найменша ж додаткова експлуатація може перетворити цю територію на пустелю[5].

---

5 Детальний огляд видів, ареалів їх проживання та екосистем, що постраждали від стихійного лиха, див. “The Consequences of the Russian Terrorist Attack on the Kakhovka Hydroelectric Power Plant (HPP) for Wildlife”, UNCG. 7 червня 2023. https://uncg.org.ua/en/the-consequences-of-the-russian-terrorist-attack-on-the-kakhovka-hydroelectric-power-station-hps-for-wildlife/.

III. Великі і малі вторгнення

Можна сказати, останнє повномасштабне вторгнення Сполучених Штатів до Мексики відбулось у 1847 році. За цим послідував договір, що утворив американський/мексиканський/індіанський палімпсест, котрий містить мене і мільйони інших людей, муху-квіткоїдку, західну болотяну сову, сича Санта-Ани, каліфорнійську комароловку та інших, здебільшого поставлених на межу виживання істот. Від того часу США не надто втручалися у справи Мексики: хіба що ЦРУ включалося у визвольні рухи 60-х і 70-х років XX ст. і катастрофічну «війну проти наркотиків», яка наводнила країну зброєю і насильством, варто згадати й нещодавні заклики правих політиків до «вторгнення в Мексику» у відповідь на нелегальну імміграцію.

Менш помітним чином армії набраних з підприємливих американців флібустьєрів[6] — спочатку прихильників рабовласництва, пізніше, ветеранів розгромлених військ Конфедерації — в пошуках колоніальних аванпостів проникали на південь аж до Венесуели. На фасаді церкви муніципального центру мексиканського штату Сонора — Каборки, де місцеві відбивалися від таких флібустьєрів, дотепер видно сліди від куль. Тоді з усіх загарбників пощадили лише одного підлітка, якого відправили назад на північ.

Протягом усієї своєї історії Мексика постійно перебувала під загрозою вторгнення чи поневолення. Те саме стосується й інших країн Америки — власне, всіх, окрім США та Канади, де колонізатори досягнули процвітання коштом корінного населення. Колись добре пристосовані до своїх земель народи Тохоно-О'одам і Кумеяай, що мешкають уздовж кордону, тепер стикаються з потрійною загрозою: зміною клімату, непрохідним кордоном і злочинністю. Гангстери та хулігани ускладнюють їм доступ до традиційних джерел їжі, а рекет, експропріація та кіднепінг здійснюються безкарно, адже правоохоронні органи чи не небезпечніші за самих злочинців. Венесуельські, гаїтянські та гватемальські біженці або чекають на шанс потрапити у США

---

6 Академ. тлум. слов укр. мови подає три значення цього слова: 1. у XVII — на початку XVIII ст. — морський розбійник; 2. у XIX ст. — північноамериканський авантюрист, що брав участь у грабіжницьких нападах на країни Південної і Центральної Америки; 3. у США — особи, що влаштовують обструкцію в конгресі. Автор використовує слово у 2 і 3 значеннях.

через офіційні пропускні пункти — Мехікалі, Сан-Луїс, Тіхуана, Ногалес — або ризикують життям на Ріо-Гранде чи в безкрайній пустелі.

Кордон — це крива. Браунсвілль, штат Техас, і його місто-близнюк Матаморос, штат Тамауліпас, розташовані на 25 градусах 90 хвилинах північної широти, а Сан-Дієго, штат Каліфорнія, і його місто-близнюк Тіхуана, штат Баха-Каліфорнія, — на 32 градусах 71 хвилині. Тож навіть за виглядом на мапі штат Техас схожий на зуб жадібного рота, що відкушує великий шмат свого південного сусіда. Якщо рухатись на північний захід від Матамороса в штаті Нуево-Леон по 100-му меридіану, який відокремлює вологий схід від посушливого заходу, то Мексику можна перетнути лише за кілька годин. До того, як сільське господарство і міська забудова перекрили річки і загнали їх під землю, Гіла, Ріо-Браво і Колорадо були прибережними магістралями, які зв'язували воєдино весь регіон. Тепер на супутникових фотографіях видно пересохлі русла, акуратні зелені кола та розчищені смуги, що свідчать про зрошуване землеробство та прикордонні споруди. Перетин кордону на офіційних контрольно-пропускних пунктах без належних документів майже неможливий, тож контрабандисти витискають останнє з беззахисних людей. Сотні нелегалів безслідно зникли в пустелі.

IV. Росія, Україна та постколоніальна непослідовність

Імперська Росія та її спадкоємці мають власну історію кримінальної географії, підприємницького насильства та корупції. Вторгнення в Україну і знищення російським урядом свого громадянського суспільства, як от нещодавнє переслідування організації «Меморіал» та арешт її співзасновника, ілюструє, що Росія не взяла на себе відповідальність за внутрішній і зовнішній колоніалізм. І то ще в кращому випадку! Українці та мексиканці відзначать спільні риси в історії своїх самобутніх культур, яскравих ідентичностей та суверенітетів під постійною загрозою зникнення так само легко, як латиш чи чеченець порозуміються з пуерторіканцем чи чаморро, що мешкають на Гуамі, або представники саамів чи бурятів знайдуть спільну мову з навахо та лакота. Важко сказати, про що нам говорить факт одночасного існування імперії ацтеків і Запорізької Січі, але фермерка Тохоно-О'одам з невеличкого господарства в Сонорі дотепер має такі ж уявлення про землю, дощі, дині і перець, як кримсько-татарська селянка, власник магазину в Ермосілло і крамар з Донецька.

V. «Ні війні»

Одним із предметів, вилучених з офісу організації «Меморіал», була наклейка з гаслом «Ні війні». Мова миру перетворилася на обертове лезо, що воно то звинувачує Росію у вторгненні, то засуджує західних постачальників зброї Україні як «розпалювачів війни». Політологи звертають увагу на «позаблоковий» дискурс і хитромудрі активні заходи на підтримку антиколоніальних рухів і рухів за громадянські права, що почалися вже за кілька років після російської пролетарської революції. Дискурс расизму, імміграції, вторгнень, як прямий, так і метафоричний — або солодша, але не менш токсична сентиментальність — містить у собі отруту. Мало, що Захід приймає українських біженців, Україна ще й має отримати від нього однозначну підтримку! Надійшов час кожному стати геополітичним аналітиком-аматором, аби з'ясувати: чи несе загрозу суверенітету поняття транскордонної спільності? А сморід вторгнення — вивітриться він за пару сотень років чи стоятиме довіку[7]?

VI. Вас вб'є якщо не спека, то вологість

У Національному центрі метеликів (Місія, штат Техас) мешкає понад 60 видів метеликів, у тому числі прекрасний мексиканський синьокрилець. У нижній частині долини Ріо-Гранде теплові індекси регулярно перевищують 120 градусів за Фаренгейтом (49 градусів за Цельсієм); в такому кліматі людина може померти від спеки за кілька годин. У Мехікалі, на кордоні Каліфорнії та Бахи, клімат сухіший, але фактична спека також сягає 120

---

7 Детальне обговорення латиноамериканських і, зокрема, мексиканських підходів до проблем громадянського суспільства, суверенітету та відповідальності див.: Sergio Gonzalez Rodriguez, The Iguala 43, Los Angeles, 2017, та Sayak Valencia, Gore Capitalism, Los Angeles, 2018.

градусів, і від теплового виснаження в долині Мехікалі регулярно гинуть люди — сільськогосподарські робітники, будівельники і люди, змушені жити просто неба через нещодавню депортацію, очікування на перетин кордону або соціальні негаразди, спричинені наркотрафіком. Варто відійти від міста, що має бодай якусь захисну інфраструктуру, як ця земля стає смертельно небезпечною для людини, яка йде пішки.

Позов проти «Ми будуємо стіну» — праворадикальної групи, яка фактично збудувала приватну тримильну ділянку прикордонного муру (й при цьому обдурила спонсорів на багато тисяч доларів) містить цілий список створених стіною проблем, як то загроза володінням Центру метеликів та дамбі Ансальдуас, що знаходиться нижче за течією. Навіть мур уряду США потребує постійного усунення наслідків впливу води і вітру, що ж казати про погано спроектовану «приватну стіну»?!

Протести Центру метеликів проти стіни і вторгнення на його територію прикордонних патрулів і озброєних дружинників зробили його ще однією мішенню для погроз і провокацій з боку правих екстремістів. Після того, як Центр знову відкрився, його директор опублікував відчайдушний відкритий лист, в якому бідкався, що організація, яка займається одними з найкрасивіших і найніжніших комах на землі, повинна «зміцнювати» свої кордони і навчати персонал зупиняти кровотечу.

VII. Немає місця — значить немає місця

Навесні 2021 року я відвідала Кітобакіто-Спрінгс, де плем'я Тохоно-О'одхам господарювало — хотілося б не у минулому часі! — протягом сотень років. Але уряд США виселив його, аби створити національний пам'ятник, нині Національний парк Орган Пайп. Зведена неподалік нього нова, нібито найсучасніша прикордонна стіна вже назбирала купи наносів та вибоїни там, де зливи повиривали глибокі яри. Пустеля Соноран — це жива екосистема, де гірські барани, вилороги, ягуари і незліченна кількість менших істот мають вільно пересуватися у пошуках води, їжі та притулку. Поки прикордонна інфраструктура складалась із поєднаних парою ліній колючого дроту стовпів, вона не завдавала великої шкоди, але нові яскраві ліхтарі, мотки колючого дроту, виїмка ґрунту та постійне патрулювання на машинах створюють зону, не придатну для життя людей і тварин. Паркова служба намагається з'ясувати, як виправити пошкодження джерел, які тепер виглядають, ніби погано збудований «водний атракціон» на чиємусь ранчо, з пошарпаною агротканиною проти бур'янів і зламаними пластиковими трубами. За кілька миль на схід, у штаті Арізона, в якості декорацій політичного театру губернатора були звели стіну з морських контейнерів[8]. Зрештою, суд зобов'язав знести її й усунути завдані пошкодження.

На Каховській дамбі вчені турбувалися про придонне життя водойми — безліч крихітних істот, які складають основу харчового ланцюга. Я з болем уявляю їхню нинішню долю, у пастці без кисню й можливості задовільнити життєві потреби. Вони не рятувалися від голоду, не тонули у підвалах своїх будинків, не вирушали у ризиковані експедиції заради чиєсь дурної ідеї. Вони не мають почуттів у звичному розумінні, і тому марно уявляти, що вони задихаються, як задихалася б я. Мабуть, для мене це занадто темні матерії.

Translated by Andriy Lysenko

---

8 Детальніше про судовий позов та реакцію Центру метеликів на узаконення тримильної стіни попри спричинені нею глибокі ерозійні шрами на березі Ріо-Гранде, що загрожують її структурній цілісності, див. на сайті Центру метеликів, доступ 9 жовтня 2024, https://www.nationalbutterflycenter.org/index.php?option=com_content&view=article&id=310&catid=9&Itemid=626.

Homok és iszap

Alisa Slaughter

2023 késő tavaszán

Az Észak-Atlanti-óceán forró, három-négy Celsius-fokkal melegebb, mint általában, a mentők pedig egy kis tengeralattjárót keresnek. Az eltűnt utazók a Titanic roncsainál vesztődtek el. A forró Atlanti-óceán és az elveszett tengeralattjáró, úgy tűnik, kapcsolódnak egymáshoz, de persze nem, csak egy mélyebb, biológiai szakterminussal élve: bentikus szinten.

Kétséges, hogy a Földközi-tengeren valaha is megtalálják azt a több mint 600 embert, akik odavesztek, amikor egy embercsempész hajó felborult a múlt héten, nagyjából ugyanakkor, amikor a Dnyeper folyót mesterségesen megárasztották, és tonnányi szennyeződés folyt be a A Fekete-tengerbe.

I. Homoki élőhelyek

Mondhatni jókedvemből veszek részt egy apró homokdűne helyreállításán Délnyugat-Kaliforniában, két hegyvonulat találkozásánál. A spanyol gyarmatosítók saját magukról nevezték el a hegyvonulatokat San Gabrielnek és San Bernardinónak. A közelben még mindig időnként folyó Santa Ana segített kialakítani azokat a dűnéket és légköri viszonyokat, ahol a Csendes-óceán, a Kaliforniai-öböl, a Sonora-sivatag és a Colorado-sivatag találkozik a hegyekkel, a szelek kiszámíthatatlan irányokba viszik a tüzeket, a klíma pedig hol nedves, hol száraz.

A munka egyszerű: eltávolítjuk az invazív mustárt, összegyűjtjük a szemetet, és cédrus tömítéseket helyezünk el, hogy a homokot ne fújja el a szél. A műanyag játékok, gumiabroncsok és szőnyegmaradványok mellett kiásunk régi, hiábavaló kísérleteket is a dűnék stabilizálására: műanyag hálókerítéseket, gyomtakaró fóliát, és most a tömítéseket, amelyek maguk nem műanyagból készülnek, bár műanyagcsíkokba vannak kötve. Mindezt egy olyan rovarért tesszük, amelyet kevesen fogunk valaha is látni: a virágszerető Delhi homokdűne légyért. Ez a szövetségi szinten veszélyeztetettként nyilvántartott faj akadályozza meg, hogy a hosszú alluviális síkot teljesen bekebelezze a régió hatalmas logisztikai központja. Az autópályák, vasúti sínek, hatalmas raktárak és hulladéklerakók által körülvett homokdűne légy minden nyáron előbukkan, és ahogy a neve is jelzi, különféle virágokat, pohánkákat, kátrányfüveket eszeget.

II. Homoki élőhelyek, keleti változat

2023 június 6-án a orosz hadsereg a Kakhovka-gáton robbantott, elárasztva ezzel a Dnyeper folyó ártereit. Óriási az emberi veszteség, katasztrofális a hatás az élő környezetre, ukrán tudósok szerint az elmúlt 100 év legjelentősebb ökológiai csapása a régióban, biológusok több életre szóló munkája lesz helyreállítani. A tájnevek saját történelmi és földrajzi sajátosságaikat tükrözik: ponto-szarmata lombhullató cserjések, euro-szibériai erdősztyepp tölgyesek, Alsó-Dnyeperi homok. A folyó emberi történelme és ősi geológiai jellege a víz, a talajtípus és az ökológiai egymásrautaltság bonyolult és biológiailag gazdag hálóját hozta létre. Az ilyen egyedi élőhelyek és fajok a legjobb körülmények között is évek vagy évtizedek alatt képesek regenerálódni; a további erőszak, invázió és kizsákmányolás őrületes pusztítást fog okozni a területen.[9]

III. Nagy és kicsi inváziók

Az Egyesült Államok 1847-ben megszállta Mexikót, ezt szokták az utolsó teljes körű inváziónak nevezni. Így jött létre az Egyesült Államok, Mexikó és mindkét ország őslakosai földjének palimpszesztje. Itt lakom én több millió emberrel

---

9 A természeti katasztrófa részletesebb hatásáról az élőhelyre, fajokra és az ökoszisztémára lásd: "The Consequences of the Russian Terrorist Attack on the Kakhovka Hydroelectric Power Plant (HPP) for Wildlife," UNCG, 7. június, 2023, https://uncg.org.ua/en/the-consequences-of-the-russian-terrorist-attack-on-the-kakhovka-hydroelectric-power-station-hps-for-wildlife/.

együtt, és ahol olyan lények, mint a virágszerető Delhi homokdűne légy, a nyugati üregi bagoly, a Santa Ana csontos hal és a kaliforniai szúnyogkapó próbálnak túlélni. Az Egyesült Államok a megszállás óta néhányszor beavatkozott Mexikó életébe: a CIA a 60-as és 70-es évek a felszabadító mozgalmait próbálta letörni, aztán ott volt a katasztrofális "drogháború", amikor fegyverekkel és erőszakkal árasztották el az országot, vagy mostanában a jobboldali politikusok felhívásai Mexikó inváziójára válaszul a kontrollálhatatlan bevándorlásra.

Még akkor is, amikor úgymond nincsen válság, a vállalkozó amerikai filibuszterek hadai – a rabszolgatartás kiterjesztésének hívei vagy később a legyőzött Konföderációs katonai erők veteránjai – egész Venezueláig hatolnak be, kolonializálható helyek után kutatva. Sonora és Caborca templomainak homlokzatán láthatóak a golyók, a helyi erők ellenállásának nyomai. A csata a helyi erők teljes győzelmével zárult, a túlélő támadókat kivégezték, kivéve egy tinédzserfiút, akit visszaküldtek északra.

Mexikó soha nem szabadult meg az invázió fenyegetésétől vagy koloniális terhétől, legalábbis a hivatalos történetírás szerint. Akárcsak a többi Amerika, az Egyesült Államokat és Kanadát leszámítva, gyarmatosítói jólétét szolgálja. A Tohono O'odham és a Kumeyaay törzsek hajdanán belakták a határ menti földeket, most a klímaváltozás, a határlezárások és a bűnözés háromszoros fenyegetésével néznek szembe. Gengszterek és gazemberek fenyegetik hozzáférésüket hagyományos élelmiszerforrásaikhoz, hivatolos vagy pusztán informális kivételes állapotot deklarálnak, melyben a zsarolás, a kisajátítás és az emberrablás könnyebben megy, mint a drogcsempészet, és ahol a rendfenntartás szinte olyan veszélyes, mint a kartellek. Venezuelai, Haiti-i és Guatemalai menekültek várakoznak menekültstátuszért a megerősített határátkelők — Mexicali, San Luis, Tijuana, Nogales — közelében, vagy életüket kockáztatják, hogy átkeljenek a Rio Grande-n vagy a végtelen sivatagon.

A határ egy görbe vonal. Brownsville, Texas és ikervárosa, Matamoros, Tamaulipas, a 25 fok 90 perc északi szélességen fekszik, míg San Diego, Kalifornia és ikervárosa, Tijuana, Baja California 32 fok 71 percen található. Könnyű elképzelni Texast úgy, mint egy fogat, egy mohó száj részét, amely éppen kiharapott egy nagy szeletet déli szomszédjából. A 100. hosszúsági kör, amely elválasztja a nedves keletet az aszállyal sújtott nyugattól, Mexikót a néhány órányi autóútra északnyugatra található Matamoros mellett, a Nuevo León államban, közel Laredóhoz szeli át. Mielőtt a mezőgazdaság és a városfejlesztés szabályozta és a föld alá terelte volna a folyókat, a Gila, a Rio Bravo és a Colorado folyók egykoron vízi autópályák voltak, amelyek összekapcsolták a régiót. Most a műholdas felvételek száraz folyómedreket és rendezett zöld köröket mutatnak, egyenes és szögletes területeket, az öntözés és a föld felszabdalásának jeleként. Hivatalos ellenőrzőpontokon szinte lehetetlen átkelni okmányok nélkül, kissé odébb viszont a csempészek jól keresnek a reményvesztett és sebezhető embereken. Emberek százai haltak meg nyomtalanul a sivatagban.

IV. Oroszország, Ukrajna és a posztkoloniális zavar

A birodalmi Oroszország örökösei folytatják büntető-földrajzi, erőszak-vállalkozói és korrupciós hagyományukat. Míg elözönlötték hadseregeik Ukrajnát, míg saját civil társadalmát üldözte a az orosz kormány — legutóbb a Memorial szervezet társalapítóját tartóztatták le és indítottak ellene büntetőeljárást — a legkevésbé sem foglalkoztatta, hogy szembenézzen saját belső és külső gyarmatosító politikájával. Ahogyan egy lett vagy csecsen volna mit beszélgessen egy Puerto Ricó-i vagy guami Chamorro lakossal, vagy egy számi vagy burját ember találhatna közös alapot a Navajo és a Lakota törzs tagjával, úgy az ukránok és a mexikóiak is találhatnának néhány közös pontot történelmükben, mint például a kulturális különbözőségek, az erős identitás, vagy a veszélyeztetett szuverenitás. Az, hogy az aztékok birodalom fennállásának időszaka egybeesett a Zaporizzsjai Szics-csel, talán keveseknek jelent valamit, de egy Tohono O'odham gazda Sonorában ugyanazt tudja a talajról és az esőről, a görögdinnyéről és a paprikáról, mint egy krími tatár az ő kis földjén; egy kis boltos ugyanúgy él Hermosillóban mint Donyeckben.

V. „Nincs háború"

Az egyik tárgy, amit elkoboztak a Memorial szervezet központjából, egy „Nincs háború"-s feliratú matrica volt. A béke nyelve forgó pengévé vált, egyik pillanatban Oroszországot vádolja a gyilkos inváziójáért, a másikban Ukrajna nyugati támogatóit nevezi „háborús uszítónak", amiért fegyvereket szállítanak. A politikai elemzők a „semleges" diskurzusra és az antikoloniális és az orosz forradalom után létrejött polgárjogi mozgalmak körültekintő támogatására hívják fel a figyelmet.

A rasszizmus, a bevándorlás és a szó szerinti vagy átvitt értelemben vett inváziók diskurzusa toxikus vagy érzelgős (ez utóbbi édesebb, de ugyanolyan mérgező), miközben ukránok ezrei menekülnek Európa felé, és jogosan számítanak támogatásra. Mindenki amatőr geopolitikai elemző kell legyen: vajon a határokon átnyúló közös terület fogalma feloldhatatlan ellentmondásban áll-e a szuverenitással? Elveszti-e egy invázió néhány száz év után az enyhe mellékízét, vagy a csonkítás örökkétartó[10]?

VI. Ha a hőség nem nyír ki, a nedvesség teszi meg

A Missionben, Texasban található Nemzeti Pillangóközpont több mint 60 fajnak ad otthont, köztük a gyönyörű mexikói kék szárnyú pillangónak is. Az alsó Rio Grande-völgyben a hőindex rendszeresen meghaladja a 120 Fahrenheitot (49 Celsius fok); ilyen éghajlatban a tűző napon az emberek néhány óra alatt meghalhatnak. Mexicaliban, a Kalifornia/Baja határ mentén a klíma szárazabb, de a tényleges hőmérséklet itt is elérheti a 120 fokot, és a hőguta rendszeresen halálos áldozatokat követel, mezőgazdasági és építőipari munkásokat, de olyan embereket is, akik azért vannak a szabad ég alatt, mert frissen kiutasították őket, vagy a határon várakoznak, vagy a drogkereskedelemmel kapcsolatos társadalmi problémák miatt szenvednek. A terület egyszerűen életveszélyes járművek és légkondicionált épületek nélkül. Persze évszázadokkal ezelőtt még megvolt a tapasztalat, hogyan kell itt élni, de — és ez a frusztráló paradoxon -—a gépek üzemeltetése és a növényzet felszámolása a fejlesztés érdekében csak még melegebbé tette.[11]

Amikor beperelték a „We Build the Wall" nevű jobboldali csoportot, akik ténylegesen építettek egy három mérföldes privát határfalat, sok-sok ezer dollárt

---

10 A latin-amerikai, főként mexikói civil társadalom, szuverenitás és felelősség kérdéseiről részletesebben lásd: Sergio Gonzalez Rodriguez, *The Iguala 43* (Los Angeles: Semiotexte, 2017), és Sayak Valencia, *Gore Capitalism* (Los Angeles: Semiotexte, 2018).

11 Az extrém hőség hatását az egészségre és a természeti környezetre, a „városi hőségsziget" jelenségét komoly kutatások dokumentálták, lásd: Polioptro Martinez-Austria és Erick R. Bandala, „Maximum Temperatures and Heat Waves in Mexicali, Mexico: Trends and Threshold Analysis," *Air, Soil and Water Research*, February 4, 2016; és Jeremy Hernandez-Rios et al., „Characterization of Patients with Guillain-Barré Syndrome in the General Hospital of Mexicali," *International Journal of Medical Students* 7, no. 3 (2019) kutatásai a mexikói térségre vonatkozóan, az egyre látványosabb összefüggések a hőség, egyenlőtlenség és várostervezés viszonylatában pedig.

csalva ki magánadományozóktól, a Pillangóközpont felsorolta az ő területeiken és az alvízi Anzalduas gáton okozott károkat.[12] Az építmény ráadásul rosszul lett megtervezve, de még maga az Egyesült Államok kormányának fala is állandó ellenőrzésre, a víz és a szél természetes hatásainak állandó kijavítására szorul.

A Pillangóközpont pere, fellépése a felfegyverzett határőrök illegális jelenléte ellen a védett területen a szélsőjobb szervezetekből további fenyegetőzéseket és megfélemlítéseket váltott ki. Miután újra elérhetővé vált a Pillangóközpont honlapja, az igazgató egy szorongó bejegyzést tett közzé, miszerint kénytelen volt biztonságosabbá tenni az oldalt, a munkatársaivel pedig elsősegélynyújtó, vérzéselállító kurzuson vettek részt, arra az esetre számítva, hogy ténylegesen is megtámadják őket.

VII. Nincs hely

2021 tavaszán meglátogattam a Quitobaquito forrást, amelyből a Tohono O'odham több száz éven át gazdálkodott — fenntartható módon, hogy ezt a sok bajt okozó melléknevet használjuk — mielőtt az amerikai kormány elűzte őket onnan, hogy egy nemzeti emlékhelyet, az Organ Pipe Nemzeti Parkot alapítsa meg. Egy új, úgymond művészi határkerítést húzott fel köréje; már most is tornyokban áll a környékén az üledék, a heves esőzések árkaiban mély sebek keletkeztek. A Sonorai sivatag élő ökoszisztéma, ahol a borz, a villásszarvú antilop, az amerikai jaguár és számtalan kisebb élőlény szabadon kell mozogjon, hogy vizet, élelmet és menedéket találjon. Amikor a határ csak néhány oszlopból és alkalmi szögesdrótból állt, nem okozott nagy kárt, de az új fényes lámpák, a borotvaéles szögesdróttekercsek, az ásatás és a folyamatos járőrözés mostanra egy életttelen zónává alakították. A Park Szolgálat próbálja kitalálni, hogyan lehetne helyreállítani a forrás károsodását, amely most úgy néz ki, mint egy rosszul megépített „vízfunkció" valakinek a birtokán, kopott gyeppel és törött műanyagcsövekkel. Hogy teljes legyen a kormányzati politikai színház, pár mérfölddel keletre, Arizona állam ideiglenes

---

12 A per részeleteit és a Butterfly Center válaszát arra a megállapodásra, hogy a Rio Grande partján három mérföldnyi falat húzzanak fel annak ellenére, hogy ezzel erodálnák a partot és megbontantanák az élőhely szerkezeti integritását lásd: https://www.nationalbutterflycenter.org/index.php?option=com_content&view=article&id=310&catid=9&Itemid=626.

falakat állított fel szállítókonténerekből. A bíróság végül elrendelte, hogy bontsák le a konténerfalat, és tegyék jóvá az okozott a károkat.

A Kakhovka gátnál a tudósok aggódnak a folyó bentikus életéért, a táplálék-lánc alapját képező apró lények sokaságáért. Szívszorító és rémisztő elképzelni a helyzetüket, ahogy a mélyben csapdába esnek oxigén nélkül, az élethez szükséges alapvető dolgok nélkül. Nem éhezés elől menekültek a vízbe, nem kockázatos kirándulásra vállalkoztak, hogy megvizsgálják valaki más elhibázott ötletét. Ők másként érzékelik a világot, hiába is próbálkozom, ők nem úgy fuldokolnak, ahogy én fuldokolnék. Talán ez túl mély nekem.

Translated by Zsuzsa Selyem

Український словник війни: воєнний час як виклик для мови

Остап Сливинський

Війна, серед усього іншого, створює ситуацію номінативного безсилля: деякі звичні слова, які ми вживаємо для опису так званої «мирної» реальності, виявляються непридатними для опису дійсності війни. Часто ідеться про інтенсивність значення. Наприклад, ми інтуїтивно відчуваємо, що словом «злочин», яким позначаємо, скажімо, шахрайство у мирний час або крадіжку цінної речі з салону автомобіля, не можна водночас називати убивство і калічення сотень людей цілеспрямованим ракетним ударом, або викрадення тисяч дітей і насильне викорінення їхньої ідентичності. Або затоплення десятків сіл і містечок і позбавлення людей можливості евакуації. Це слово тут непридатне, його значення надто слабке, і епітети в цьому випадку не допоможуть. Ми потребуємо якогось іншого слова, хоч і розуміємо, що назвати — означає вже певною мірою нормалізувати; якщо мова — дім буття, то все, що ми називаємо, ми неначе вносимо у свій дім. Але іншого виходу немає: наше буття творимо не лише ми, але й ті, хто приходить, щоб нас убити. Ми маємо назвати те, що несе нам загибель, щоб вчасно розпізнати його і знешкодити. Нам потрібні слова для найстрашнішого.

Іноді ми йдемо шляхом, яким пішов мешканець Львова, правник Рафаель Лемкін, автор терміну «геноцид», і створюємо слова. Використовуємо фрагменти (уламки) існуючих слів, щоб назвати нашу поламану реальність: так виникають терміни на кшталт «рашизму», який нещодавно був офіційно визнаний Верховною Радою України як назва політичного режиму в РФ.

Іноді ми «позичаємо» слова: так в Україні на позначення «шефів» окупаційних «адміністрацій» часто вживається термін, що походить з лексикону Третього Райху — «ґауляйтер». Цей термін неточний, але відображає тенденцію: щоб назвати реальність, в якій ми опинилися, звертаємося до найтемніших сторінок історії людства.

Із відчуття неспроможності мови виник проєкт «Словник війни», що його я започаткував навесні 2022 року. Неможливість ні повірити в реальність того, що відбувається довкола, ні підібрати для нього слова змушувала мене почуватися професійно непридатним, адже слова, тексти, письмо були тим, з чим, як мені здавалося, я вмію працювати найкраще. Згодом я зрозумів важливу річ: ця реальність вже приходить з певними словами, вона не мовчазна. І, хоч мова її часто плутана, уривчаста, треба її слухати, щоб хоч щось зрозуміти. І я почав слухати.

Моїми співрозмовниками в перші тижні повномасштабного вторгнення були люди, що прибували на Львівський вокзал евакуаційними потягами з півночі, півдня, сходу України. Я як волонтер був серед перших, з ким вони зустрічалися відразу після прибуття. Дехто з вимушених переселенців був мовчазним, але багато з них — можливо, більшість — відчувши себе у відносній безпеці, починали розповідати. Часто контакт із дорослими вдавалося налагодити через дітей – дорослі слідом за ними вступали у невимушену розмову.

Часто розповіді були схожими у своїй основі, з повторюваними структурами: «почули вибухи — зрозуміли, що війна», «швидко пакувалися — були збентежені, шукали можливість виїзду», «важко було їхати евакуаційним потягом», «не маємо контакту з родичами чи друзями, не знаємо, що робити далі», «переймаємося за того, хто під окупацією, або за того, хто на фронті», тощо. Ці сюжетні структури сильні, але позбавлені чогось, що пронизало б нас емоційно і вирвало з якогось жахливого, але повторюваного досвіду. І мені було дуже важливо знайти ті елементи, які були б унікальними в історії, які індивідуалізували б її і водночас підкреслювали її універсальність, промовистість навіть поза конкретним контекстом. Точніше, то не був свідомий пошук: цю роботу великою мірою за мене робила моя власна пам'ять, бо саме ці фрагменти найглибше і найвиразніше запам'ятовувалися.

Часто це були фрагменти, які будувалися на якомусь образі чи асоціації. Хоча переважно моїми співрозмовниками були люди, далекі від літератури чи мистецтва, вони нерідко мислили художньо, шукали вдалих порівнянь. Прагнучи виразити щось, що їх особливо вразило, потрясло, вони вдавалися до мови образів.

Коли у моїх записах накопичилася певні кількість таких фрагментів монологів, я почав шукати форму, яка могла б їх об'єднати. І знайшов її дещо несподівано: то була форма словника. Власне, в кожному фрагменті можна було виділити якесь найважливіше слово (слово-образ, слово-поняття), довкола якого будувалася оповідь. До того ж форма словника, організованого за абеткою, дозволяла зробити всі оповіді рівними, вільними від метасюжетів чи хронології.

Одним із джерел такої ідеї був поетичний цикл Чеслава Мілоша «Світ. Наївні поеми», який він писав в окупованій нацистами Варшаві. У цьому циклі він ніби намагається реставрувати первісні значення слів, спотворені, затерті війною. Це — назви конкретних речей («Дорога», «Ґанок», «Сходи») або абстракцій («Віра», «Надія», «Любов», «Тривога»). Мені ж ішлося про дещо інше: показати, як війна змінює значення слів, як у контексті війни слова набувають додаткового значення-тіні, обростають новими асоціаціями або й взагалі змінюють свою семантику.

Так, «ванна» набуває значення укриття і рятує оповідачку під час обстрілу; «зірка» — це фігура, яку утворюють клейкі стрічки, наліплені на віконну шибу, щоб вберегти скло від розлітання в разі вибуху; «мангал» — це вже не атрибут відпочинку, заміського пікніка, а інструмент виживання за умов відсутності електрики й газу. Те саме стосується й абстракцій: «краса» стає не просто недоречною, а й небезпечною, бо несе для жінки загрозу зґвалтування; «радість» стає засобом спротиву; «тиша», замість заспокоювати, тривожить, бо може ховати у собі небезпеку; «сни» лякають, бо за ними неминуче йде перспектива прокидання.

Навесні, коли я почав волонтерити в прихистках для тимчасових переселенців, я отримав нагоду для довших бесід, і свідомо почав скеровувати співрозмовників до думок про слова, які вони вживають. І зрозумів, що навіть у людей, далеких від лінгвістики, може прокинутися якийсь філологічний інтерес, і вони відчувають слова як ключі до реальності. Так у розмові з жінкою, що повернулася з евакуації з Польщі, народилася рефлексія про „pokój" — слово, яке польською означає і «кімната», і «мир». Або про польське словосполучення „pod gołym niebem" («під відкритим небом»): на думку оповідачки, воно більше пасує українському небу, яке є справді «голим», незахищеним.

Ідея «Словника війни» викликала такий інтерес, що в процесі роботи над проєктом до нього долучалися інші співавтори і співавторки, які надсилали свої історії про слова; а ще — ілюстратори, перекладачі, видавці. «Словник війни» став справжнім соціально-культурним проєктом, до того ж міжнародним. Станом на сьогодні книга, яка містить понад 80 історій, видана вже українською, німецькою, польською, словацькою мовами; плануються видання в Чехії, Румунії, Грузії, Південній Кореї, Японії, США; фрагменти публікувалися литовською, латвійською, угорською, італійською та іншими мовами. Існують дві версії ілюстрацій до «Словника», а також театральні та музичні адаптації цих текстів.

Звичайно, доки триває війна і пам'ять про неї, проєкт не може бути завершений. У моїх планах — продовження «Словника», історії до якого я буду збирати на деокупованих і прифронтових теренах, серед військових і людей, що пережили окупацію, депортацію.

The Ukrainian Dictionary of War: Wartime as a Challenge to Language

Ostap Slyvynsky

War, among other things, creates a situation of nominative impotence: some of the usual words that we use to describe so-called peaceful reality turn out to be unsuitable for describing the reality of war. It is often about the intensity of meaning. For example, we intuitively feel that the word "crime" we use to designate, say, fraud in peacetime or the theft of a valuable item from the interior of a car cannot apply to the killing and maiming of hundreds of people by a targeted missile strike, or the abduction of thousands of children and the obliteration of their identity, or flooding dozens of villages and towns and preventing evacuation. "Crime" is inappropriate here, its meaning is too weak, and intensifiers will not help in this case. We need some other word, although we understand that to name means to normalize to a certain extent; if language is the house of being, then everything we name, we bring home. But there is no other way out: we create our existence, but it is also created by those who come to kill us. We have to name what brings us destruction in order to recognize it in time and neutralize it. We need words for the worst.

Sometimes we follow the path taken by the lawyer Rafael Lemkin, a resident of Lviv, who coined the term "genocide," and create words. We use fragments (debris) of existing words to name our broken reality: this is how terms like *ruscism*[1] arise.

---

1 This Ukrainian neologism combines the words "Russia" and "fascism." Its similarity to the word "racism" is accidental, but emphasizes its toxicity. (Translators' note.)

The Verkhovna Rada of Ukraine voted to use it to describe the political regime in the Russian Federation.

Sometimes we borrow words: for example, in Ukraine, a term originating from the lexicon of the Third Reich is often used to denote the "chiefs" of the occupation "administrations"—*Gauleiter*. This term is imprecise, but reflects a trend: to name the reality in which we find ourselves, we turn to the darkest pages of human history.

I started the *Dictionary of War* project in the spring of 2022, after I perceived this impotence of language. The impossibility to believe in the reality of what is happening, combined with the inability to choose the words for it, made me feel professionally unsuitable, because words, texts, writing were what I thought I could work with best. Over time, I realized an important thing: this reality already comes with certain words, it is not silent. And, although reality's language is often confused and fragmentary, you have to listen to it in order to understand at least something. And I started listening.

My interlocutors in the first weeks of the full-scale invasion were people who arrived at the Lviv station on evacuation trains from the north, south, and east of Ukraine. As a volunteer, I was among the first people they met immediately upon arrival. Some of the forcibly displaced people were silent, but many of them—perhaps the majority—began to talk once they felt relatively safe. Often it was possible to establish contact with the adults through the children—the adults followed them into a casual conversation.

Often, the stories were similar at their core, with repeated structures: heard explosions, and we understood that it was war, packed quickly, we were confused, looked for an opportunity to leave, it was difficult to take the evacuation train, we have no contact with relatives or friends, we don't know what to do next, we worry about someone who is under occupation or someone who is at the front. These plot structures are strong, but they lack something that would pierce us emotionally and pull us out of some terrible but repetitive experience. And it was very important for me to find those elements that would be unique in each story, that would individualize it and at the same time emphasize its universality, eloquence even, outside of a specific context. More precisely, it was not a conscious search: this work was largely done for me by my own memory, because it was these fragments that I remembered deeply and vividly.

Often these fragments were built on some image or association. Although my interlocutors were mostly people who were far from literature or art, they often thought artistically and looked for good comparisons. Trying to express something that particularly struck and shocked them, they resorted to the language of images.

When a certain number of such fragments of monologues accumulated in my notes, I began to look for a form that could unite them. And I found it somewhat unexpectedly: it was the form of a dictionary. Actually, in each fragment it was possible to single out the most important word (word-image, word-concept), around which the story was built. In addition, the form of the dictionary, organized in alphabetical order, made it possible to make all stories equal, free from metaplots or chronology.

One of the sources of such an idea was Czeslaw Milosz's poetic cycle *World: Naive Poems,* which he wrote in Nazi-occupied Warsaw. In this cycle, he seems to be trying to restore the original meanings of words, distorted and erased by the war. These are the names of concrete things ("Road," "Porch," "Stairs") or abstractions ("Faith," "Hope," "Love," "Anxiety"). I was thinking about something else: to show how war changes the meaning of words, how in the context of war words acquire an additional shadow meaning, grow new associations, or even change their semantics.

Thus, *bathroom* acquires the meaning of shelter that saves the narrator during shelling; a *star* is a figure formed by adhesive tapes stuck on the window pane to prevent the glass from flying apart in the event of an explosion; a *grill* is no longer associated with recreation, a country picnic, but becomes a tool for survival in the absence of electricity and gas. The same applies to abstractions: *beauty* becomes not only inappropriate, but also dangerous, because it carries the threat of rape for a woman; *joy* becomes a means of resistance; *silence,* instead of calming, disturbs, because it can hide danger; *dreams* are frightening because they are inevitably followed by the prospect of waking up.

In the spring, when I started volunteering at shelters for temporary migrants, I had the opportunity to have longer conversations, and I consciously began to guide my interlocutors to think about the words they use. And I realized that even people who are far from the formal study of language can awaken to it and feel words as keys to reality. Thus, in a conversation with a woman who returned from evacuation from Poland, a reflection was born about *pokój*—a word that means both "room" and "peace" in Polish. Or about the Polish phrase *pod gołym niebem* ("under the open sky"): in the narrator's opinion, it fits better with the Ukrainian sky, which is truly "bare," unprotected.

The idea of the *Dictionary of War* aroused such interest that, in the process of working on the project, other co-authors joined it and sent their stories about words; and also illustrators, translators, publishers. The *Dictionary of War* has become a real socio-cultural project, moreover, an international one. As of today, the book, which contains more than eighty stories, has already been published in Ukrainian, German, Polish, and Slovak languages; further editions are planned in the Czech Republic, Romania, Georgia, South Korea, Japan, the United States; fragments were published in Lithuanian, Latvian, Hungarian, Italian, and other languages. There are two versions of illustrations for the *Dictionary*, and theatrical and musical adaptations of these texts have been created.

Of course, as long as the war and the memory of it continue, the project cannot be completed. My plans include a continuation of the *Dictionary*, stories I will collect in de-occupied and near-front areas, among military personnel and people who survived the occupation and deportation.

Translated by Alisa Slaughter and Julia Sushytska

Дві історії

Андрій Содомора

Флейта

На дні тісного дворика дотанцьовують весілля. Одне за одним гаснуть вікна, і лиш одне, на верхньому поверсі, ще бореться із сутінню вересневого вечора. Внизу шурхотять підошви. Гупає бубон, а здається, що то якийсь вайлуватий здоровань, сп'янівши, не знаходить виходу з кам'яної пастки — б'є та б'є важкою стопою об кам'яні плити двору. На його незграбне гупання хрипким сміхом озивається акордеон, а далі — знову вперте й важке: гуп-гуп . . .

Час од часу подає голос флейта — уже вкотре злітає вгору схожими на кам'яні цямрини стінами. Та не дотягується до густо-синього чотирикутника, де яскравіє одинока зірка, — обривається, тихне, пірнувши в парку глибінь колодязя, так само раптово, як і вихопилася звідти . . .

У кімнаті, де ще не погасло світло, — напівсутінь. Лише на письмовому столі, мов окреслене циркулем, — сліпуче коло настільної лампи: низько, мовби вичитуючи щось, вона хилиться над білим аркушем паперу. Тонюсінькою тасьмою — димок від цигарки, що тліє на попільничці. Більше нікого. Хіба що, на єдиній тут картині, — темна сильветка жінки, яка відходить засніженою алеєю у глибину парку. А ще — той, хто в тіні, хто, думаючи про щось своє, дивиться за звичкою на постать, що віддаляється, маліє, а все ж не полишає засніженого простору . . .

Того разу флейта зметнулася тоді, коли далека зірка ось-ось мала торкнутися верхнього контуру кам'яниці. Ковзнула вертикаллю стіни, від якої вже лиш на волосинку була мерехтлива цятка на небі. Якраз тією вертикаллю, де під самим зрізом будинку світилося прихилене вікно. Вклала в цей злет усю свою снагу, усю жагу простору. І бриніла в її голосі пам'ять про ті далекі часи, коли хіба що Вітер, володар простору, налітавшись у високостях, під вечір, коли замерехтіла зоря, тулився до очеретин, і вони, шелеснувши, озивались на його доторк солодким багатоголоссям. Ще тоді, у дні вічної Весни . . .

Смужка диму, що на мить мовби застигла у спрямованому на аркуш паперу пучкові світла, враз колихнулася, захвилювалась, наче стрічка в руці вправної танцюристки. Той, хто залишався в тіні, підійшов до вікна. Зауважив, що й фіранка затремтіла . . . І тут його пройняло відчуття, що, крім нього й жінки, яка віддаляється, у кімнаті побував ще хтось третій, та тільки одну мить . . . Зачинивши вікно, вимкнув лямпу. Темрява, що переповнювала схоже на колодязь подвір'я, враз захлюпнула кімнату. А за вікном — посвітлішало: за перехрестям рами, де щойно віддзеркалювалася пітьма, сіріла стіна . . .

Десь у глибинах Всесвіту, з кінцем осіннього рівнодення, схитнулося сузір'я Терезів. Та чи схитнулося? Адже рух — неперервний. Своїм шляхом, як і перед віками, пливе й та зірка, яка щойно зазирала у двірколодязь, де гупав бубон, шкірився акордеон і тужним голосом пробивалася до чотирикутника високого неба неспокійна флейта. Певно, й пробилася б за останнім злетом, якби їй на дорозі, під самим зрізом муру, не стало прочинене, ще не погасле вікно . . .

Танець

Гей ви, музиченьки, заграйте ми чардаш,
Най я си погулям тот остатний раз.

Давно б забулась та сумна, з давніх днів, історія, давно б зітерлася з пам'яті, якби не тих кілька штрихів — у кольорах: білий кожушок, червона хустина, така ж довкола стану палахка крайка . . .

Гора з горою не сходиться. Нива з нивою — зійшлися. Більша дотяглася до меншої. Лишень межа ще їх ділила. А щоб і її не лишилося, щоб із двох зробилась одна велика нива, треба було, щоб зійшлись іще двоє людей: господарський син, що на більшій ниві, — з донькою того, хто на скромнішій газдував.

Силою гнали її до шлюбу — рідний батько і той, за кого мусила вийти заміж, аби не дробилося поле. Поки священик єднав їх в одне ціле, — калабаньку сліз наплакала в церкві перед вівтарем: побіч стояв нелюб, а десь у світі, при війську, служив той, кого обрала душею, — її любий.

Незадовго по весіллю він прийшов із війська. У неділю грали до танцю троїсті музики. Птахою шугнула з хати — до нього. Пустилися в танець — наче в обійми одне одному попадали. Поки грали музики, доти й не випускав її з обіймів. А ті грали, як ніколи, до самої ночі грали — для них: «Думала, що там повмираємо обоє . . .» Гупав, мов розгарячене серце, бубон, зойкала скрипка, жалощами розсипалися цимбали . . . Казав їй, що йде на війну, що вже не вернеться . . .

Чоловік, коли стемніло, гнав її додому буком — ген через усе село. Бив день і ніч, щоб його любила, щоб забула того, хто прийшов з війська й пішов далі — у світ . . . Можливо, піддалася б, як і всі інші, кому не поталанило, можливо, й скорилася б долі. Можливо . . . Якби — не ті музики, що так їм правдиво грали до того недільного — вітального й прощального, довгого й короткого, як саме життя, — їхнього танцю . . . Залишилася, якою була — ставною і гордою: «Шоби мав мене забити, то все єдно би-м'го не любила».

Білий кожушок, червона хустина, така ж довкола стану палахка крайка . . . А ще — нива, що й повесні, хоч і зеленіла, та не світила їй, як було, надією — розлукою чорніла . . .

Two Stories

Andriy Sodomora

The Flute

In the depths of the cramped courtyard, a wedding dances itself out. Windows go successively dark, and only one, on the topmost floor, battles on against the twilight of the September evening. Down below, soles shuffle. A *bubon* bangs, and it sounds as though some lumbering, drunken Samson is stuck in a stone prison—the thwack of heavy footfalls on the yard's stone slabs. In answer to his oafish crashing—the hoarse laugh of an accordion and then, once again, that stubborn, ponderous banging.

Now and again, a flute's voice wafts in—soars up the walls, which resemble the stone shaft of a well. Yet it never reaches the deep-blue rectangle where a lonely star pulses—it breaks off, goes quiet, plunging back into the airless depths of the well just as suddenly as it sprang forth . . .

In the one room where the light is still on, it's nearly twilight. Only there on the desk, as if drawn by a compass—a blinding orb of lamplight: A lamp bows low over a white sheet of paper, as though scanning for something. The thinnest little thread—smoke from a cigarette that's smoldering in an ashtray. No one's there anymore. Save for the dark silhouette of a woman, following a snowy path into the depths of a park, in the room's only picture. And there's also someone in the room's shadows, someone lost in introspection, glancing out of habit at the receding figure—getting smaller, but still not vanishing from the snow-filled expanse . . .

One last time the flute's voice shot upward just as the faraway star was about to touch the upper contours of the stone building. It sailed up the wall, a hair's breadth from that shimmering dot in the sky. Along the same axis, right under the eaves, a window gleamed, slightly ajar. The flute put all its energy, all its desire for open space into that ascent. In its voice trilled the memory of a distant time when Wind—ruler of space, tired of soaring in the sky—would nestle alone in the reeds as the evening's first star appeared in the sky, and the reeds would rustle back, responding to his touch with sweet polyphony. Back in the days of eternal Spring . . .

The thread of smoke that for a moment had seemed immobile in the lamplight illuminating the paper was suddenly tossed about, twirling like a ribbon in the hands of a nimble dancer. And that someone in the shadows approached the window. He noticed that the curtain was trembling, too . . . Suddenly he was struck by the feeling that, besides him and the receding woman, there was a third person in the room, but only for a moment . . . He closed the window and turned off the lamp. The darkness spilling out of the well-like courtyard flooded the room. But outside, things looked brighter: Through the gridded pane that just now had reflected darkness, the wall shone gray . . .

Somewhere in the depths of the universe near the end of the autumnal equinox, one side of the constellation Libra dipped down. But wasn't it dipping all along? Motion, after all, is continuous. Continuing on its course was the same star which, drifting along for centuries, had just peered into the courtyard-well, where the *bubon* banged, the accordion cackled, and, in a sorrowful voice, the restless flute tried to break through to that lofty rectangle of sky. And probably it would have broken through in this final flight if on its way, at the topmost edge of the wall, no window had stood ajar, and no light had shone through it . . .

The Dance

"Hey you, musicians, play me the csárdás,
One last dance before I go."

(From a Lemko song.)

That sorrowful story of days past would have been forgotten long ago, it would have passed from memory, were it not for a few vivid details: a white *kozhushok* coat, a red kerchief, and a woven sash of the same fiery color.

Mountains don't come together but two fields did, once—a larger one extending toward a smaller one. Only a boundary line divided them. To do away with that as well, two people had to come together: the son of the wealthy farmer on the large field and the daughter of the man who farmed the more modest one.

She was forced into the marriage—by her own father and by the man she had to marry to make the field whole. At the church altar, as the priest was joining them as one, she shed a river of tears: Beside her stood a man she didn't love, while the one her heart had chosen—her beloved—was somewhere out in the world, serving in the military.

Shortly after the wedding, he returned from the army. That Sunday, a trio of musicians played at a dance. She took flight from her house like a bird—to see him. They started dancing, as though falling into one another's embrace. So long as the music played, he didn't release her from his arms. And the trio played like never before, well into the night—just for them: She thought they'd both die there . . . The *bubon* banged like an impassioned heart, the violin howled, the cymbals shook with pity. He told her he was going back to the war. That he wouldn't return.

After nightfall, her husband drove her home with a beech switch—for the whole village to see. He beat her day and night so that she'd love him and forget that other man who'd returned from the army, then moved on—into the world. Maybe she would have given in, like so many unlucky girls had, and submitted to her fate. Maybe . . . Were it not for those musicians, who'd played for them so fervently throughout that Sunday dance, of homecoming and of parting, as prolonged and brief as life itself—*their* dance. She remained the same as ever—slender and proud. "He can kill me—I'll still never love him," she'd say.

A white *kozhushok*, a red kerchief, and a woven sash of the same fiery color. And also a field that, while verdant in spring, didn't shine with hope, as it once had—but further darkened her separation.

Empty Forms, Infinite Becoming: Freedom to Be Ordinary

Julia Sushytska

A key danger to all beings, including the earth, is the systematic destruction of the tissue that enables human beings to become human. This tissue is slowly weaved in spaces opened up by democratic institutions and works of art. It allows humans to change—to search for and become more than who they are "naturally," but it is fragile: vulnerable to neglect, violence, and cynical manipulation. In "The Power of the Powerless" Vaclav Havel notes that authoritarian regimes force their subjects to choose between being a hero or being a coward. Such a choice is not abstract or trivial, especially if one has small children or elderly parents. Havel wrote this from Soviet-controlled Czechoslovakia when many of his readers lived in non-authoritarian societies. Today the space outside authoritarian societies is rapidly shrinking, and the danger that all human beings might be cornered into Havel's dichotomy seems more urgent than half a century ago.

> *edizēsamēn emeōuton.*[1]

This is an aphorism by Heraclitus of Ephesus, and its translation into English requires adding at least two more words: "I searched for myself." Ukrainian, like Greek, needs only two: *Shukav sebe*. The second word, *emeōuton*, means "myself," but the verb *edizēsamēn* is more difficult to translate into English. It is an aorist—a

---

1 DK 101.

simple past tense—of *dizēmai,* to seek out, look for, inquire, desire. This past tense does not convey the idea of repetition or duration (the imperfect "I was searching"), or of a completed action (the perfect "I have found"). Herodotus uses this verb in the context of trying to understand an oracle that has already been asked for and given. The oracle speaks in enigmas, and *dizēmai* refers to the process of deciphering or clarifying obscure words.[2]

Even the oracle's unambiguous pronouncements—"You will kill your father and marry your mother"—must not be accepted and acted on thoughtlessly. They require work. "I searched for myself" is neither a straightforward, unambiguous truth claim, nor a purposefully misleading statement. It is an enigma that only *I* can try to work out. Nobody can be born or die for me, and nobody can understand for me. Enigmatic words make this truth more palpable.

Commenting on Heraclitus's aphorism, Charles Kahn concludes: "Self-knowledge is difficult because the human is divided from itself."[3] This is a fortunate difficulty—a happy fault in the sense of the Easter Vigil's *Exsultet*: "O happy fault, O necessary sin of Adam, which gained for us so great a Redeemer!" Heraclitus's text draws attention to the idea that this search is possible *because* a human being is "divided" from themself. I am never complete or fully present, and this means that I can change: become more than I am; become human.

***

Heraclitus's "I searched for myself" can illuminate a key civilizational element that is threatened today. Merab Mamardashvili identified it from the margins of both Western Europe and Russia—from the in-between of these two colonial powers. In "European Responsibility," a lecture delivered in 1988 at an international symposium on the cultural identity of Europe, Mamardashvili defined "Europe" as the process of complexity and diversity.[4] "Europe" is not a geographical place or a

---

2 Charles Kahn, *The Art and Thought of Heraclitus* (Cambridge: Cambridge University Press, 1999), note 84, 309.

3 Ibid., 116.

4 See Merab Mamardashvili, "European Responsibility," in *A Spy for an Unknown Country: Lectures and Essays by Merab Mamardashvili,* ed. and trans. Alisa Slaughter and Julia Sushytska (Stuttgart: ibidem, 2020), 57–62.

geopolitical entity, but a process, and he emphasized that "Europe" could happen in, for instance, Japan, and fail to happen in France.

In 1988, in Paris, Mamardashvili used the vocabulary of the Greco-Roman world and Christianity to identify two important aspects of the process called "Europe." An atheist, he referred to Christian symbols and events from the Bible to explain abstract ideas. He often layered the terminology from different "language games" for pedagogical reasons, but also to push back against Soviet ideology, as well as acknowledge some of his favorite writers, such as Dante. Mamardashvili realized that he does not belong to Europe, even if he loves and intimately knows its philosophy and literature and understands its institutions. He opens "European Responsibility" by acknowledging his position as an outsider, but he sees his non-belonging as epistemologically advantageous: "I wanted to talk about the concepts that formed within me on the basis of the experience of a young person, the personal experience of a human being who was born outside Europe, who lived in the hinterland and became conscious there of his country's history and culture. The lesson that I derived from my experience is that I had a privileged vantage point to see what a European cannot see."[5]

From this position of greater objectivity Mamardashvili identifies two key aspects of "Europe-as-process": the rule of law and "the inner voice or word,"[6] the process of becoming conscious through a conversation with oneself. This notion of consciousness emerges during Hellenism, but is traceable to Homer and Socrates: "every Greek hero essentially carries on a conversation with himself, and in doing so he thinks his thoughts, feels his emotions, and debates courses of action."[7] I can understand what I think and feel only if I separate myself from myself who thinks and feels it. For instance, when angry I distance myself from myself who is angry in order to understand what I actually feel and why. This separation is the first, necessary step in transforming myself—in becoming more than my angry self.

In Homer this separation is fully embodied—it is not an intellectual discussion. Instead, I have the "organs of consciousness," and I am in conversations with them: *kêr*, "the "heart" or even the "stomach"; *êtor*, the "heart" as the seat of emotions

---

5 Mamardashvili, "European Responsibility," 57–58.

6 Ibid., 59 and 60.

7 Barbara Cassin, "The Greek for 'Consciousness': Retroversions," in *Dictionary of Untranslatables: A Philosophical Lexicon*, ed. Barbara Cassin and Emily Apter (Princeton, NJ: Princeton University Press, 2014), 176.

and intelligence, and especially *thumos*—the entrails, the diaphragm, the lungs.[8] Mamardashvili's returns to an embodied sense of the inner voice by emphasizing human tissue that is created during these conversations. He also underscores that this work can and needs to be done by me—my personal responsibility: "It is necessary to walk without external help, following the inner voice, without counting on guarantees, and with all of that appears a disruptive and discomfiting element."[9] Mamardashvili also emphasizes the element of risk that this conversation with oneself involves: "I step aside, that is, I have to break connections, shed my skin, my family, my education, my country (homeland), because while connected to them, I treat them as self-evident, or true."[10] The aspect of "Europe-as-process" that Mamardashvili calls "inner voice" is a safeguard against essentializing—associating myself too closely or permanently with an ethnic group, a nationstate, or a culture.

This second aspect of "Europe" does not entail individualism or solipsism, but it is clearly different from collectivism or *sobornost'*. "Europe-as-process" avoids extremes because of the first aspect—the rule of law. Mamardashvili also identifies it as the idea that "a finite form can carry the infinite."[11] A key example of such finite form is the *agora*—a place where I can meet others and converse with them on equal footing because no one is above the law. Mamardashvili notes that forms like the *agora* or civil society should be left empty of specific content, even the most just, otherwise they will become yet another container for ideology. "Democracy's formalism is better than the clear content of a just regime. A just regime is a chronic demonstration, whereas formal democracy is a cultural structure that provides you with an interval, in which you can become a human being and find out what you want and what you really think, because we don't know it on our own."[12] The *agora* opens up an interval for the search because it puts me in conversation with others and helps me to distance myself from myself. The *agora*

---

8 Ibid. The notion of inner voice becomes prominent during Hellenism and gradually loses its bodily aspect.

9 Mamardashvili, "European Responsibility," 60–61.

10 Mamardashvili, "Lecture 6," in *A Spy for an Unknown Country: Lectures and Essays by Merab Mamardashvili*, 89.

11 Ibid., 59.

12 See lecture 9 of Mamardashvili's *Lektsii o Pruste*, in Merab Mamardashvili, *Psikhologicheskaia topologiia puti (M. Prust. "V poiskakh utrachennogo vremeni")* [The psychological topology of a path (M. Proust, "In search of lost time")], vol. 2 (Moscow: Merab Mamardashvili Foundation, 2014), 195.

also facilitates other forms that can carry the infinite: the novel, the university, the free press.

It is crucial that "Europe" is founded on not one, but on two principles, and there is tension between them: the divided, incomplete self and the possibility to encounter others in a space ruled by law. In this, "Europe" differs from an authoritarian regime where an Ivan or a Vladimir fills all forms with ideological content and in this way forecloses the possibility of the search. A fractured self and an empty form of the *agora* are not contradictory, but there is a tension between them—only *I* can understand, and I can do it only if I shed my affiliations; to understand I need to be in conversation with others on the *agora*, with the laws placed in the middle.

The first element of "Europe" is the level playing field—an open, horizontal space governed by laws (however imperfect). From the *agora* I can go in search of myself. I can become human without having to be a hero or face moral annihilation. I still need to make a considerable effort, but it doesn't have to be the heroic-tragic effort. The *agora* facilitates the creation of the artificial tissue that makes a human being human.

***

Tissue is intricate by definition. The English word comes from the Latin *texo* (to join or fit together; to interweave, intertwine; to construct, make, fabricate), and is related to the Greek *tiktō*, to beget.[13] Human beings can make the world more textured—more intricate, more complex. They can give texture to their own selves. Mamardashvili points out that "it is not the ethical prohibition of denunciation that makes me understand that I should not denounce, and makes me unable to denounce—this is what I call the tissue."[14] Through a laborious process I change myself in such a way that it becomes physically impossible for me to become an informant. If I don't lie, it is not because of knowing (intellectually) that I ought not do it, but because of an embodied inability. In Ukrainian this idea is reflected at the idiomatic level: *iazyk ne povertaiet'sia*—my tongue does not turn (for instance, to tell a lie). If I cannot inflict harm on someone, or steal, it is

---

13 Charlton T. Lewis, Charles Short, *A Latin Dictionary* (Oxford: Clarendon Press, 1879).
14 Lecture 10 in Mamardashvili, *Psikhologicheskaia topologiia puti*, 228.

because *ruka ne pidnimaiet'sia*—my hand does not lift to do it. Notice the nuance: in English one would say "I cannot raise my hand against him," but in Ukrainian my body becomes the actor—the subject of a sentence.

The artificial tissue that I can create or grow, transforms my body. It enabled Varlam Shalamov to survive the Gulag. The narrator of his harrowing short story "Day Off" notes that the only thing that "had not yet been crushed by fatigue, sub-zero temperatures, starvation, and endless humiliations" was "favorite verses by other poets, which by some miracle I could remember here, a place where everything else was forgotten, discarded, expelled from the memory."[15] This tissue, weaved by Shalamov and the poets he read, enabled him to survive the camps. Another extreme example is a Ukrainian journalist, Stanislav Aseyev. For twenty-eight months he was a political prisoner in a (still functioning) FSB-run concentration camp in the Russian-occupied Donetsk. In his preface to the memoir that recounts and reflects on his experiences he observes that, to write this book, "I had to survive. To survive I had to know that I need to write it."[16] The artificial process of writing over the years transformed Aseyev in such a way that he did not lose his humanity while his torturers tried to destroy it. In the extreme circumstances of gulags or wars it is easy and natural to act in inhuman ways, and difficult to rise above what one is being reduced to by violence. The *agora* protects us from having to test the durability of our personal tissue in the way Shalamov and Aseyev had to do it. Living in a society structured around the rule of law opens the possibility of being a human being without having to choose between heroism and cowardice.

***

The tissue that enables me to become human takes time and effort to weave, and is easily destroyed. It took Marcel Proust about fourteen years to write *In Search of Lost Time*, and during this time he did little else. In a sense, it took Proust all of his life, and also the lives of his parents, teachers, and many writers who preceded him.

---

15 Varlam Shalamov, *Kolyma Stories*, trans. Donald Rayfiled (New York: NYRB, 2018).

16 Stanislav Aseyev, *"Svitlyi shliakh": Istoriia odnogo kontstaboru* (Lviv: Vydavnytstvo starogo leva, 2020), 224. Translated by Zenia Tompkins as *The Torture Camp on Paradise Street* (Cambridge, MA: Harvard Library of Ukrainian Literature, 2024).

On May 24, 2024, Faktor-Druk, the second largest publishing house in Ukraine with approximately 3,000 titles in print, was bombed by Russia.[17] Faktor-Druk published about a third of the books, and about 50 percent of the textbooks in Ukraine. "The missiles launched from S-300 surface-to-air system hit the printing house, destroyed over 50,000 books and printing equipment. It also killed seven employees and injured 22."[18] Two months before this a missile destroyed another printing facility, and more than fifteen other publishing houses suffered damage since Russia began full-scale invasion in 2022.[19]

This is a direct attack on a form that sustains the effort of becoming human. The news and images of burned books are immediately spread around the globe, and yet the global community has not stopped Russia from this violence. This raises Russia's violence to another level: it is destroying not just a nation, but the possibility of the search for oneself. Russia is intentionally and systematically targeting the first aspect of "Europe-as-process"—the rule of law, and this is affecting all of us, even if we are not aware of it.

Still, the agora and the search are not only fragile, but also resilient. The empty finite forms that allow for infinite possibilities are fragile because they are not filled with ideological content, but this emptiness also makes them durable. This happy fault constitutes our advantage. Russia has the power to burn books, but it cannot stop me in my search. It can try to undermine the rule of law, but cannot prevent me from creating new ways to sustain it.

---

17 "Russian Forces Hit Vivat Publishing House in Kharkiv," *Ukrains'ka pravda*, May 23, 2024, https://www.pravda.com.ua/eng/news/2024/05/23/7457225/#:~:text=Founded%20in%202013%2C%20Vivat%20publishing,%2C%20Oksana%20Moroz%2C%20and%20others.

18 Dominic Culverwell, "What will Russia's Attack on Kharkiv Printing House Mean for Ukraine's Publishing Industry?," *Kyiv Independent*, May 28, 2024, https://kyivindependent.com/russias-attack-on-kharkiv-printing-house-puts-publishing-industry-at-risk/.

19 See "U Kharkovi raketa znyshchyla drukarniu. Ie zagybli i dev'iatero poranenykh," Chytomo, March 20, 2024, https://chytomo.com/u-kharkovi-raketa-znyshchyla-drukarniu-ie-zahybli-j-dev-iatero-poranenykh/.

Порожні форми, нескінченне становлення: Свобода бути звичайним

Юлія Сушицька

Найбільша небезпека для всього живого, включно із Землею, полягає в систематичному нищенні тканини, яка дозволяє людині ставати людиною. Ця тканина повільно виплітається у просторах, утворених демократичними інституціями та мистецтвом. Вона дозволяє нам змінюватися — шукати і ставати чимось більшим, ніж ми є «від природи». Але наскільки ж вона крихка! Вразлива до байдужості, насильства і цинічних маніпуляцій. У статті «Сила безсилих» Вацлав Гавел зазначає, що авторитарні режими змушують своїх громадян обирати між героїзмом і малодушністю. Й якщо у нас маленькі діти або літні батьки, цей вибір втрачає навіть тінь абстракції чи самоочевидності. Хоча сам Гавел писав це з контрольованої СРСР Чехословаччини, для багатьох його читачів авторитаризм тоді не сприймався як особиста загроза. Відтоді тиск авторитарних суспільств на світ різко зріс, тож небезпека того, що всі ми виявимось загнаними в кут Гавелової дихотомії значно серйозніша, ніж півстоліття тому.

edizēsamēn emeōuton[20].

20 DK 101.

Аби передати цей афоризм Геракліта Ефеського англійською, доведеться використати щонайменше ще два слова: "I searched for myself". Українській мові, як і грецькій, достатньо двох: Шукав себе. Друге слово, *emeōuton*, означає «сам», а от дієслово *edizēsamēn* перекласти складніше. Це аорист — простий минулий час дієслова *dizēmai*, — шукати, видивлятись, запитувати, бажати. Цей минулий час не передає ідею повторення або тривалості (недоконаний вид, «я шукав»), або завершеної дії (доконаний вид, «я знайшов»). Геродот використовує це дієслово в контексті спроби розтлумачити оракула, який вже дав відповідь на поставлене йому запитання. Оракул говорить загадками, й *dizēmai* позначає процес розшифрування або роз'яснення темних слів[21].

Навіть очевидні пророцтва оракула на кшталт — «Ти вб'єш свого батька і одружишся з матір'ю» — не можна сприймати бездумно. Над ними слід працювати. «Шукав себе» — це не пряме, однозначне висловлювання якоїсь правди і не навмисне введення в оману. Це загадка, яку здатний розгадати тільки *я*. Ніхто не може народитися чи померти за мене, і ніхто не може зрозуміти за мене. Таємничі слова тільки підкреслюють цю істину.

Коментуючи афоризм Геракліта, Чарльз Кан підсумовує: «Самопізнання є складним, бо людина відокремлена від самої себе»[22]. Й це щаслива складність — щаслива помилка в сенсі *Exsultet* Літургії Пасхи: «О щаслива провина, о необхідний гріх Адама, які заслужили на такого величного Визволителя!». Вислів Геракліта вказує на те, що пошук можливий саме тому, що людина «відокремлена» від самої себе. Я ніколи не є цілісним або приявним уповні, а отже, спроможний мінятися: робитись більшим, ніж є; ставати людиною.

***

У світлі Гераклітового «шукав себе» якнайкраще проступає ключовий елемент цивілізації, що він нині опинився під особливою загрозою. Мераб Мамардашвілі знаходив його на маргінесі як Західної Європи, так і Росії — власне, поміж цими двома імперськими утвореннями. У лекції «Європейська відповідальність», прочитаній у 1988 році на міжнародному симпозіумі з культурної ідентичності Європи, Мамардашвілі визначив «Європу» як

---

21 Charles Kahn, The Art and Thought of Heraclitus, Cambridge, 1999, — с. 309.
22 Там же, с. 116.

практику ускладнення та урізноманітнення.[23] «Європа» — це не географічне місце чи геополітична одиниця, а зусилля, тож «Європа» може виникнути, скажімо, в Японії, і не відбутися у Франції.

У 1988 році в Парижі Мамардашвілі використовував лексику греко-римського світу та християнства, щоб визначити два важливі аспекти процесу під назвою «Європа». Сам невіруючий, для пояснення абстрактних ідей він блискуче використовував християнські символи та Біблійні сюжети. Філософ вдавався до різних «мовних ігор» не лише з педагогічних міркувань, а й в якості противаги радянській ідеології і шани своїм улюбленим авторам, як от Данте. Мамардашвілі усвідомлював, що не належить до Європи, навіть якщо любить і глибоко знає її філософію та літературу, розуміє її інституції. «Європейську відповідальність» він починає з визнання свої позиції стороннього, при цьому підкреслюючи її епістемологічну перевагу: «Я хотів би сказати кілька слів з приводу тих ідей, які з'явились у мене на основі досвіду — особистого досвіду людини, яка народилася не в Європі, жила у провінції і там пізнавала історію своєї країни та її культури. Урок, який я виніс з мого досвіду, що маю привілейовану точку огляду, що вона дозволяла побачити ті речі, котрі європейці можуть не бачити»[24].

З цієї позиції більшої об'єктивності Мамардашвілі виділяє два ключові аспекти «Європи як практики»: верховенство права та «внутрішній голос або слово»[25], процес усвідомлення через розмову з самим собою. Це поняття свідомості сформувалося в добу еллінізму, але бере початок від Гомера та Сократа: «кожний грецький герой, властиво, веде розмову із собою, завдяки цьому думає свої думки, відчуваючи свої емоції та обговорюючи шляхи дій»[26]. Я можу зрозуміти, що думаю і відчуваю, тільки якщо відокремлю себе від себе, хто думає і відчуває. Наприклад, коли я гніваюсь, то аби зрозуміти, що і чому я насправді відчуваю, я мушу дистанціюватись. Це відокремлення

---

23 Див. Merab Mamardashvili, European Responsibility, // A Spy for an Unknown Country: Lectures and Essays by Merab Mamardashvili, *ред. і пер.* Alisa Slaughter and Julia Sushytska, ibidem, 2020, — сс. 57–62.

24 Там же, сс. 57–58.

25 Там же, сс. 59 і 60.

26 Barbara Cassin, The Greek for "Consciousness": Retroversions", // Dictionary of Untranslatables: A Philosophical Lexicon, ред. Barbara Cassin і Emily Apter, Princeton, 2014, — с. 176.

є першим, необхідним кроком у моєму перетворенні – в тому, щоб стати чимось більшим, ніж розлюченим я.

У Гомера це розділення втілене, це не інтелектуальна дискусія. Розмову я веду зі своїми «органами свідомості»: *kêr*, «серцем», ба навіть «шлунком»; *êtor*, «серцем» як місцем розташування емоцій та інтелекту, а, головне, *thumos* — нутрощами, діафрагмою, легенями[27]. Мамардашвілі повертається до сенсу втіленого внутрішнього голосу, наголошуючи, що тканина людського твориться під час розмов. Він наголошує, що цю роботу можу і мушу виконувати тільки я — ніхто інший за неї не відповідає: «Слід йти без зовнішньої підтримки, слідуючи внутрішньому слову, не розраховуючи на гарантії, і з цим з'явиться елемент пертурбації, елемент тривоги і елемент, який творить історію»[28]. Філософ нагадує й про ризикованість цієї розмови з самим собою: «Я відступив вбік – тобто я маю вискочити зі зв'язків, зі своєї звичної шкіри, зі своєї сім'ї, зі своєї освіти, зі своєї країни (батьківщини), адже, допоки я в них, я їх приймаю як самоочевидне або істинне»[29]. Аспект «Європи як практики», який Мамардашвілі називає «внутрішнім голосом», є запобіжником від есенціалізації — надто тісного ототожнення себе з етнічною групою, національною державою чи культурою.

Цей другий аспект «Європи» не призводить до індивідуалізму чи соліпсизму, але він чітко відрізняється і від колективізму чи соборності. Подібних крайнощів «Європа як зусилля» уникає через перший аспект, що його Мамардашвілі зве як верховенством права, так і ідею, що «кінцева форма може бути носієм нескінченного»[30]. Ключовим прикладом такої обмеженої форми є *agora* — місце, де я можу зустрічатися з іншими і спілкуватися з ними на рівних, бо ж ніхто не вище закону. Філософ зазначає, що такі форми, як агора чи громадянське суспільство, мають бути позбавлені конкретного змісту, навіть найсправедливішого, інакше вони стануть ще одним вмістилищем ідеології. «Формалізм демократії кращий, ніж чіткий зміст будь-якого справедливого устрою. Чому? Бо справедливий устрій є хронічним мітингом, а формальна

---

27 *Там же.* В добу еллінізму поняття внутрішнього голосу акцентується, поступово втрачаючи свій тілесний аспект.

28 Mamardashvili, *A Spy for an Unknown Country,* — сс. 60–61.

29 Там же, 89. Пер. за Мераб Мамардашвили, Психологическая топология пути, М., 2014, — с. 131.

30 Mamardashvili, *A Spy for an Unknown Country,* — с. 59.

демократія — це культурна структура, яка дає тобі інтервал, у якому ти можеш стати людиною; зокрема, завдяки розумінню, чого ти хочеш і що ти насправді думаєш»[31]. *Агора* відкриває інтервал для пошуку, тому що ставить мене в розмову з іншими і допомагає дистанціюватися від самого себе. *Агора* також сприяє іншим формам, спроможним нести нескінченне: роману, університету, вільній пресі тощо.

Вкрай важливо, що «Європа» заснована не на одному, а на двох принципах і між ними існує напруга: розділене, неповне «я» та можливість зустрітися з іншими в просторі, де панує закон. Цим «Європа» відрізняється від авторитарного режиму, де Іван чи Володимир наповнюють усі форми ідеологічним змістом і таким чином усувають можливість пошуку. Роздроблене «я» і порожня форма агори не суперечать один одному, але між ними існує напруга: лише я можу зрозуміти, і я можу це зробити, лише якщо позбудуся своєї приналежності; щоб зрозуміти, мені потрібно опосередковане законами спілкування з іншими на *агорі*.

Першим елементом «Європи» є рівний ігровий майданчик — відкритий горизонтальний простір, де панують закони (хай і недосконалі). З *агори* я можу піти на пошуки себе. Можу стати людиною, оминаючи вибір між героїзмом і моральним знищенням. Звичайно, зусиль доведеться докласти чималих, але не конче героїко-трагічних. *Агора* сприяє створенню штучної тканини, яка робить людину людиною.

***

Тканина є складною за визначенням. Англійське слово *tissue* походить від латинського *texo* (з'єднувати або поєднувати; переплітати, плести; конструювати, робити, виготовляти) і споріднене з грецьким *tiktō* — породжувати[32]. Людина може зробити світ більш текстурованим – складнішим, диференційованішим. Вона може надати текстуру власному я. Мамардашвілі зазначає, що «не через етичну заборону доносу до мене прийшло розуміння того, що неможна доносити, і в мені виникла нездатність

---

31 Див. лекцію 9 // Мераб Мамардашвили, Лекции о Прусте, // Мераб Мамардашвили, Психологическая топология пути, М., 2014, — т. 2, с. 195.

32 Charlton T. Lewis, Charles Short, *A Latin Dictionary*, Oxford, 1879.

доносити. Ось це я називаю тканиною»[33]. Через трудомісткий процес я змінюю себе так, аж мені стає фізично неможливо стати сексотом. Якщо я не брешу, то не тому, що знаю (інтелектуально), що не слід цього робити, а через втілену неспроможність. В українській мові це уявлення відображене на ідіоматичному рівні: *язик не повертається* (наприклад, збрехати). Якщо я не можу комусь заподіяти зла або вкрасти, то тому, що *рука не піднімається* це зробити. Зверніть увагу на нюанс: англійською мовою говориться "I cannot raise my hand against him" (Я не можу підняти руку на нього), а українською суб'єктом речення виступає саме моє тіло.

Штучна тканина, яку я можу створити або виростити, трансформує моє тіло. Це дозволило Варламу Шаламову вижити в ГУЛАГу. Наратор його жахливої новели «Вихідний день» зазначає: «Єдине, що не було пригнічене втомою, морозом, голодом і нескінченними приниженнями», — це «чужі улюблені вірші, які дивним чином трималились там, де все інше було давно забуте, викинуте, вигнане з пам'яті»[34]. Ця тканина, виткана Шаламовим і поетами, яких він читав, дозволила йому вижити в таборах. Ще один яскравий приклад – український журналіст Станіслав Асєєв. Протягом 28 місяців він був політичним в'язнем у концтаборі ФСБ (все ще діючому) в окупованому Росією Донецьку. У своїй передмові до мемуарів, де він розповідає і розмірковує про цей досвід, він зауважує, що для написання цієї книги «мені довелося вижити. Щоб вижити, я повинен був знати, що мені потрібно це написати»[35]. Штучний процес письма протягом багатьох років змінив Асєєва так, що він не втратив своєї людяності, хоч як його мучителі намагалися її знищити. В екстремальних обставинах ГУЛАГів чи воєн легко і природно діяти нелюдськими способами, і важко піднятися над тим, до чого нас зводить насильство. *Агора* захищає від необхідності перевіряти на міцність власну тканину так, як це довелося зробити Шаламову та Асєєву.

---

33 Лекція 10 // Мераб Мамардашвили, Лекции о Прусте, // Мераб Мамардашвили, Психологическая топология пути, М., 2014, — т. 2, с. 228.

34 Варлам Шаламов, Выходной день, // Варлам Шаламов, Воскрешение лиственницы, рассказы, Москва, 1959, — с. 118.

35 Станіслав Асєєв, «Світлий шлях»: історія одного концтабору, Львів, 2020, — с. 224. Англійський переклад: Zenia Tompkins, пер., The Torture Camp on Paradise Street, Cambridge, 2024.

Життя в суспільстві, побудованому навколо верховенства права, дозволяє бути людиною без необхідності вибирати між героїзмом і малодушністю.

***

Тканина, яка дозволяє мені стати людиною, потребує часу і зусиль для її ткання, і легко руйнується. Для написання «У пошуках втраченого часу» Марселю Прусту знадобилося близько чотирнадцяти років, і на це пішли майже всі його сили. У певному сенсі, на це пішло все його життя, а також життя його батьків, вчителів і письменників, які йому передували.

24 травня 2024 року «Фактор-Друк», друге за величиною видавництво в Україні, що видавало близько 3 000 найменувань, було розбомблене Росією[36]. «Фактор-Друк» видавав близько третини книжок і близько 50% підручників в Україні. «Ракети, випущені із зенітно-ракетного комплексу С-300, влучили у друкарню, й знищили понад 50 000 книг та друкарське обладнання. Загинуло семеро працівників, ще 22 отримали поранення»[37]. За два місяці до цього ракета знищила ще одну друкарню, а від початку повномасштабного вторгнення Росії у 2022 році постраждали понад 15 інших видавництв[38].

Це пряма атака на форму, яка підтримує зусилля стати людиною. Новини та світлини спалених книг миттєво розлетілися світом, але світова спільнота не зупинила Росію. Це піднімає насильство Росії на інший рівень: вона знищує не лише іншу націю, а саму можливість пошуку себе. Росія навмисно і систематично націлена на перший аспект «Європи як практики» — верховенство права, і це впливає на всіх нас, навіть якщо ми цього не усвідомлюємо.

---

36 «Росіяни вдарили по друкарні видавництва Vivat у Харкові», // «Українська правда», 23 травня 2024, https://www.pravda.com.ua/eng/news/2024/05/23/7457225/#:~:text=Founded%20in%202013%2C%20Vivat%20publishing,%2C%20Oksana%20Moroz%2C%20and%20others.

37 Dominic Culverwell, “What will Russia’s Attack on Kharkiv Printing House Mean for Ukraine’s Publishing Industry?”, // *Kyiv Independent*, 28 травня 2024, https://kyivindependent.com/russias-attack-on-kharkiv-printing-house-puts-publishing-industry-at-risk/.

38 Див. «У Харкові ракета знищила друкарню. Є загиблі й дев’ятеро поранених», // Читомо, 20 березня 2024, https://chytomo.com/u-kharkovi-raketa-znyshchyla-drukarniu-ie-zahybli-j-dev-iatero-poranenykh/.

Втім, *агора* і пошук не лише крихкі, але й стійкі. Порожні кінцеві форми, які допускають нескінченні можливості, крихкі, оскільки не наповнені ідеологічним змістом, але ця ж порожнеча надає їм міцності. Ця щаслива вада є нашою перевагою. Росія може спалювати книжки, але вона не може зупинити мене в моєму пошуку. Вона може спробувати підірвати верховенство права, але не може перешкодити мені створювати нові способи його підтримки.

Translated by Andriy Lysenko

Гуманітарний коридор

Ігор Померанцев

Щодня у моєму підкасті «Гуманітарний коридор» слова лунають всуміш із сльозами. У мене в студії побіля мікрофону стоїть літрова пляшка води, а поруч лежить пачка паперових хустинок. Історії біженців схожі одна на одну: перші вибухи, вимкнені ліфти, пробіжка з 14-го поверху у підвал, опісля відбою — повернення на своїх двох назад на 14-ий. Тлум на вокзалі, діти, що загубили батьків, собаки, які зірвалися з повідця. Три доби у потягах до польського або румунського кордону. Добрі люди — волонтери, чужа, але гостинна земля. Для багатьох біженців — це перший закордон: до війни на подорожі не було часу і грошей.

Я почуваюся рентгенологом, який працює без свинцевого фартуха або захисної стіни. Щодня мене опалює чужим горем. Мій «коридор» робиться гігантським, у чверть Європи. Це схоже на біблійну картину: коридором тягнуться жінки і діти. Чоловіки залишились воювати. У жінок в одній руці три торбинки, що у них умістилося все їхнє життя, у другій — рука хлопчика або дівчинки, котрі розмазують по щоках шмарклі і сльози. Під пахвою у дитини коробка з-під взуття, а там — кошеня або щеня. [. . .]

Я вислухав і передав в ефір вже півсотні історій і півлітра сліз. Але й у мене є власна історія. Їй півсотні років, але вона не втрачає актуальности. Вона також про насильство. І джерело цього насильства те ж, що й сьогодні: моя батьківщина. У 1976 році мене заарештували за читання «заборонених книжок». Мені не встромляли під нігті голок, не мочились в обличчя. Але пригрозили: «На тебе чекає табір, а там ми, на жаль, не все контролюємо». Радянська людина мого покоління добре розуміла цю мову: у таборі тебе «опустять» [. . .]. Ймовірно, майор і підполковник вже померли — земля їм дротом. Але їхні діти й онуки сьогодні повернулись в Україну на танках і бомбардувальниках. Повернулись на світанку, не стукаючи у двері, розривами бомб і ракет.

***

Я почуваюсь зайвим: люди, з якими я розмовляю, здійснюють вчинки, діють, борються, а я тільки говорю. Але іноді мені здається, ніби я поруч із ними: у підвалі, на вокзалі, на кордоні.

Я запитую:

— Катерино, ви знялися у головній ролі в стрічці «Моя бабця Фанні Каплан». Це насамперед історія кохання, але ж Каплан увійшла в історію іншим: замахом на Леніна у 1918 році. Яке у вас ставлення до цього вчинку?

— [. . .] якось вночі була повітряна тривого, і моя донька Віра сховалась у шафу. Ми схопили всіх дітей і побігли у бомбосховище під театром. Там було багато дітей, знайомих акторів, домашніх тварин [. . .]. Діти складали пазли з поламаної плитки. Актори демонстрували фокуси. Бомбардування закінчилось. Й один музикант зіграв на ксилофоні пісеньку, а тоді сказав: «Дякую! Мирної вам ночі!».

Я наполегливо повертаюсь до головного запитання:

— Катерино, але зараз ви б натиснули курок?

Катерина ледь чутно вимовляє: «так» [...]

***

Наприкінці лютого 2022 року російський посол у Швеції в інтерв'ю газеті «Aftonbladet» сказав: «Вибачте за вираз, але нам насрати на західні санкції». Особисто я його не пробачаю. [...]

У 1995 році під час першої чеченської війни я розмовляв з біженкою з Грозного Фатімою. Я поставив їй стандартне журналістське запитання: «Що вас вразило найбільше? Танки? Бомби?» Вона подумала. А тоді ніяково сказала: «Російські солдати заходили в порожні будинки і . . . випорожнювались в наші постілі. Перепрошую. Так, випорожнювались, накривали гівно ковдрою, знову полегшувались і накривали всю купу подушками. Ми не могли повірити».

У березні 2022 року біженка Наталка з Чернігівської області на моє запитання: «Що під час окупації вас вразило найбільше?», відповіла: «Вони займали наші хати і срали у ліжка».

Ті російські солдати, які «полегшувались» в Чечні, були вбиті, повернулись контуженими або мирно померли у власних постелях. Але їхні сини або онуки прийшли в Україну і повторили те, чому їх навчили батьки і діди. У переліку військових злочинів немає параграфу: «справляти нужду у ліжка громадян окупованої держави». В міжнародному суді подібні випадки розслідуватись не будуть. Але сморід залишиться надовго. Тож екологам буде чим зайнятись.

***

«О 17:20 мені відірвало руку разом з годинником. Цей час на ньому й залишився», — розповідав український солдат, що знімався у документальній стрічці «Ампутація» в 2017 році. [. . .] 24 лютого 2022 року українські годинники знову зупинились. За останні два з половиною місяці я записав для радіо десятки біженців з України. Вони повторюють і повторюють:

— Перший вибух я почула о п'ятій ранку. Мій пес загавкав. Але тільки після другого вибуху я зрозуміла, що це війна.

— Коли я почула перші вибухи, то подумала, що хтось підриває петарди. Ми сіли в машину, час зупинився, а ми їхали і їхали. [. . .]

Мої співрозмовники, не змовляючись, кажуть, що 24 лютого годинники мовби зупинились й увімкнувся інший час — час війни, а попередній час повернеться лише тоді, коли війна закінчиться. Війна — інша країна. Там все інакше. Там живуть в іншому часі і просторі. [. . .]

Я бачу кадр: відірвана рука з годинником завмерла у повітрі. Лейтенант хрипить українською. Я чую його голос: «Нас не подолати».

***

Празький тележурналіст, що знімав мене для передачі «Вавилон», спитав, де я почуваюся вдома. Я замислився і не зміг одразу відповісти. Точніше, я відповів, але якось змазано, хоча й щиро: мовляв, я людина-транзит, змінив п'ять країн, півдюжини міст і почуваюся вдома тільки в готелі. [. . .] Про старі церкви кажуть — «намолені». Дім також треба «надихати». Це праця кількох поколінь. Невпинна праця. XX століття радикально змінило уявлення про дім, самий образ дому. Революціонери у коричневих і чорних сорочках, у комісарських шкірянках не залишили від дому каменя на камені. Мільйони людей переселились у котловани соціалістичних будівництв, в бараки Дахау, у газові камери Освенціма, а вцілілі розійшлись по комуналках. Цілі народи виселялись з будинків предків, а опустілі приміщення заселялись безликими масами. На початку п'ятдесятих років минулого століття в міжнародному праві з'явився термін «переміщені особи» (DP), що їх рахунок йшов на мільйони. Це були люди, котрих Друга світова війна позбавила дому і батьківщини. [...]

Без жодної патетики, але й не без гордості я можу назвати народ, до якого належу вже сорок з гаком років. Мій народ — це переміщені особи, політ- і просто емігранти, біженці, бродячі пси Європи. Я — патріот.

***

На дев'ятий день війни на Вацлавській площі зібралось сто тисяч демонстрантів. Багато, дуже багато студентів. А кажуть, що родинна пам'ять — міф. Але ж хіба міф не частина життя? На тротуарі поруч із пам'ятником св. Вацлаву вмостився жебрак із прапором кольору неба і пшениці на плечах. Він бурмотів (з чеським акцентом): «Слава Україні», «Слава Украіаіні». Це була його зоряна година. [...]

***

Дякую, німецький професоре Ясперсе, що відкрили нам термін «погранична ситуація» (Grenzsituation). Розширимо його межі. Не лише людина, а й нація може опинись під загрозою й у смертельній небезпеці. Ми бачимо зараз, як героїчно бореться за існування тіло України. Для письменника «погранична ситуація» розповсюджується й на територію мови. Письменництво передбачає скрайню близькість з мовою. Смерть — також край. Де пролягає межа однієї мови та її сусідів? Чи може одна мова загрожувати іншій? Ще б пак. Прикладів — безліч: києм, палицею, обіймами. [...] У фіналі роману [Джойса «Портрет митця замолоду»] Стівен приходить до висновку, що ірландська версія англійської — почерпнута мова і приймає рішення використати її як інструмент для виразу полоненої душі Ірландії.

Я згадав цей епізод [. . .], коли несподівано для себе прочитав в есеї британського письменника, мого сина Пітера, що пишучи англійською, він відчуває вантаж імперських гріхів і готовий нести його.

Джойс — тепло. Пітер — гаряче. Все моє свідоме — дозахідне — життя минуло в Україні. Минуло, але все ж залишилось у ній. Російська завжди була для мене рідною. Війна — це погранична ситуація не лише для носіїв мови, а й для самої мови. Убивство народу — це ще й вбивство мови.

Свій підкаст я веду російською. Дотепер це lingua franca для колишніх радянських людей. У 1976 році в КДБ ця мова врятувала мене. Я був російським письменником, а отже, «старшим братом». Мене неможна було звинувати в українському націоналізмі, а «націоналізм» в Україні тоді був найважчим гріхом: за нього давали сім років таборів і п'ять років висилки.

Я письменник і люблю рідну мову. Сьогодні моя любов в силі, як і раніш, однак стала важкою, драматичною. Зло — поліглот. Воно говорить сотнею мов. Але серед них є в нього й улюблені, можна сказати, рідні. В німецького поета Пауля Целана, що з ним я пов'язаний одним містом — Чернівцями (Czernowitz), є класичний вірш про зло. Він називається «Фуга смерті». Ключовий рядок у ньому: «Смерть — це майстер з Німеччини». Сьогодні смерть змінила мундир і нашивки. Тепер смерть розмовляє російською, і нас пов'язує спільна мова. Але я не віддам смерті жодної частки, жодного пробілу між словами.

P.S. Свій останній роман «Поминки за Фіннеганом» Джеймс Джойс написав на семидесяти мовах, включно з англійською. Трикратне «Ура!» впертому ірландцеві.

Translated by Andriy Lysenko

Humanitarian Corridor

Igor Pomerantsev

Every day in my podcast "Humanitarian Corridor," we speak through tears. I keep a liter bottle of water and a pack of tissues ready near the microphone. The stories of refugees all resemble each other: the first explosions, the disabled elevators, the sprint from the fourteenth floor to the basement, and, after the "all clear," climbing back up. Refugees crowd the station just like in war movies, the parentless children, leashless dogs, compassionate volunteers, a strange but hospitable land. For most refugees, this is their first time abroad. Before the war there was neither time nor money for travel.

I feel like a radiologist working without a lead apron or a protective wall. Every day, I am scorched by another person's grief. My "corridor" is huge, a quarter of Europe. It's an almost biblical picture: women and children trudge down a hall. The men stayed back to fight. In one hand, the women have three shopping bags carrying everything from their previous lives. In the other, a little boy or girl, snot and tears smeared on their cheeks. The child carries a shoebox with some little kitten or puppy inside. [. . .]

I have listened to and broadcasted fifty stories and a half liter of tears. However, I too have my own story. This is a story that is half a century old, but it has not lost its relevance. Mine too is about violence. The source of this violence is the same source as today: my motherland. In 1976, I was arrested for reading "forbidden books." They didn't stick needles under my nails or pee in my face, but they threatened. "There is a camp waiting for you, and in it, unfortunately, we can't control everything." Soviets of my generation understood this language well: in the camp, they will make you the bitch, make you a *petukh* ("rooster") and put you to work in the "chocolate factory." The major and lieutenant colonel must have already died—may they rest on a bed of barbed wire. But today their sons and grandsons return to Ukraine in tanks and airplanes. They return at dawn, without a knock on the door, with the explosions of bombs and rockets.

***

I feel superfluous: the people that I talk with *do* things, act, fight. And I'm only talking. But sometimes it seems to me that I'm with them; in the basement, at the station, at the border.

I ask, "Ekaterina, you starred in the film *My Grandmother Fanny Kaplan*. Above all, this is a love story, but Fanny Kaplan went down in history for another performance: the 1918 attempted assassination of Vladimir Lenin. How do you feel about this?"

"[. . .] Yes, one night there was an air raid warning, and my daughter Vera hid herself in a wardrobe. We took all the children and ran to the bomb shelter below the theater. There were a lot of children, a lot of our actor friends, pets. [. . .] The children put together puzzles out of broken tile. The actors performed tricks. The bombing stopped, and one musician played a tune on the xylophone, and afterwards said: 'Thank you! Have a peaceful night!'"

I persistently returned to the main question:

"But Ekaterina, now would you pull the trigger?"

Ekaterina, almost inaudibly, said "yes." [. . .]

***

In mid-February of 2022, in an interview with the magazine *Aftonbladet,* the Russian ambassador to Sweden said: "Apologies for the language, but we don't give a shit about Western sanctions." Personally, I don't forgive him. [. . .]

In 1995, at the time of the First Chechen War, I spoke with Fatima, a refugee from Grozny. I gave her my standard journalist question: "What startled you the most? The tanks? The bombs?" She thought for a bit, and, embarrassed, said: "The Russian soldiers entered empty houses and . . . they pooped in our beds. Sorry. Yes, they pooped, covered the shit with a blanket, pooped again and covered the whole mess with pillows. We couldn't believe it."

In March of 2022 a refugee, Natalka from Chernihiv Oblast, responded to my question "What startled you the most during the occupation?" that "They occupied our houses and shat in our beds."

Those Russian soldiers who "pooped" in Chechnya were either killed or returned shell-shocked, or peacefully passed away in their own beds. But their sons or grandsons came to Ukraine and repeated what fathers and grandfathers taught them. The list of war crimes does not include the paragraph "to relieve oneself in the bed of citizens of an occupied state." Such instances will not be investigated in the international court. But the stench will remain for a long while. And so, environmentalists will have something to keep them busy.

***

"At 17:20 my hand was ripped off along with my watch. The time remains with them," a Ukrainian soldier said in the documentary *Amputations*, in 2017 [. . .] On February 24 of 2022, Ukrainian watches again stopped. Over the past two and a half months I recorded dozens of refugees for the radio. They repeat, over and over.

"I heard the first blast at five in the morning. My dog was barking. Only after the second blast did I realize that this was war."

"When I heard the first blasts, I thought that someone had set off firecrackers. We got into the car, time stopped, and we drove and drove." [. . .]

My interviewees independently arrive at the same conclusion: the clock stopped on February 24 and another time began—the time of war. The earlier time will return only when the war ends. War is another country. Everything is different there. They live in another time and place. [. . .]

I see a scene: a severed hand with a watch frozen in midair. The lieutenant wheezes in Ukrainian. I can hear his voice. "They won't defeat us."

***

A broadcaster from Prague who filmed me for the television program *Babylon* asked where I feel at home. I thought this through and wasn't able to answer straightaway. My answer was vague, but also sincere: I'm a man on the move.

I've changed countries five times, cities half a dozen times. I feel at home only in hotels. [. . .] They say old churches are prayed into existence. Similarly, you make a house by breathing inside it. This is the work of several generations. The twentieth century radically altered our conception of home, the very shape of it. Revolutionaries in brown and black shirts, in commissars' leather overcoats, dismantled the home stone by stone. Millions of people relocated to the foundation pits of socialist construction sites, the barracks of Dachau, the gas chambers of Auschwitz; the survivors scattered to communal apartments. Entire nations were expelled from the homes of their ancestors, and their deserted houses were settled by faceless masses. At the beginning of the 1950s, the term "Displaced Persons" (DP) entered international law; they counted in the millions. These were people who were dispossessed of their homes and homelands by the Second World War. [. . .]

Without pathos, but also with pride, I am able to name the nation to which I have belonged now for some forty years. My nation is the displaced persons, the political migrants and the ordinary immigrants, the refugees, the stray dogs of Europe. I am a patriot.

***

On the ninth day of the war, 100,000 demonstrators assembled on Wenceslas Square in Prague. There were so many students. And they said that family memory is a myth! But isn't myth a part of life? Perched on the pavement near the statue of Saint Wenceslas, a beggar wore a flag with the colors of wheat and the sky. He muttered (in a Czech accent): "Slava Ukraini, Slava Ukrainini!" This was his finest hour. [. . .]

***

Thank you, German Professor Jaspers, for giving us the term "limit situation" (*Grenzsituation*). Let's expand its horizons. Not only people, but nations too may find themselves facing a threat or mortal danger. We see now how heroically the body of Ukraine fights for existence. For writers, the "limit situation" extends into the territory of language. Writing requires the utmost intimacy with language. Death is also a limit. Where is the border between a language and its neighbors? Can one language endanger another? Of course. For example: if not by washing, then by scrubbing, and then squeezing. [. . .] At the end of the novel [Joyce's *A Portrait of the Artist as a Young Man*], Stephen comes to the conclusion that the Irish version of English is derivative, and makes the decision to use it as a tool to express the captive soul of Ireland.

I remembered this passage [. . .] when to my surprise I read my son Peter's essay. He, a British writer writing in English, said that he felt the burden of imperial sin and is ready to bear it.

Joyce is warm, but Peter is warmer. I spent my entire conscious pre-Western life in Ukraine. That life is spent, but it remains in Ukraine. Russian has always been my native language. War takes the speakers of a language to their limits, but also limits the language itself. The murder of a nation is also the murder of its language.

I host my podcast in Russian. It is still the lingua franca for former Soviet people. In 1976, this language saved me from the KGB. I was a Russian writer, which meant "older brother." I could not be accused of Ukrainian nationalism, and "nationalism" was then the most serious sin in Ukraine: a "nationalist" was sentenced to seven years in the camps and five years in Siberia.

I am a writer, and I love my native language. Today my love still endures, but it has become difficult, dramatic. Evil is a polyglot, it speaks hundreds of languages. But even it has its favorite languages, its "native" languages. The German poet Paul Celan, whose city of origin Chernivtsi (Czernowitz) is also mine, has an exemplary poem about evil. It is called "Death Fugue." Its crucial line is "Death is a master from Germany." Today, death has changed its uniform and stripes. Now, death speaks Russian; a common language binds us. But I will not yield a single pronoun to death, not even a space between words.

P.S. James Joyce wrote his final novel, *Finnegans Wake*, in seventy languages, including English. A triple "Hurray!" for the stubborn Irishman.

Translated by
Alisa Slaughter, Julia Sushytska, and Garrett Howard

О.П.

Acknowledgments

It is difficult to enumerate our obligations as we assemble a book of literary documents developed in a country at war. We should acknowledge Ukraine itself, which tolerated and even welcomed our strange project during the anxious summer of 2023—we certainly should, but the formulation is elusive.

With that debt still unresolved, we would like to unreservedly thank all of our contributors and translators. They provided their work and ideas, and the book would not exist without their participation. Special thanks are due to Andriy Lysenko, who translated virtually all of the contributions into Ukrainian, Oleh Panasiuk, whose paintings are integral to this book's design, and to Yale historian Marci Shore, who helped us develop the project at every stage, introducing us to many key participants and supporters.

For material support during the summer institute, we extend sincere thanks to Hryhoriy Baran and The Renaissance Foundation. Thanks to Yevhenii Monastyrskyi who put us in touch with the foundation. We are profoundly grateful to the Jan Michalski Foundation for their generous support of this series, and thank Vera Michalski, Cecilia Galindo, and the entire staff at Michalski for their patience and support for our project. We are grateful to Academic Studies Press, particularly Alessandra Anzani and Kate Yanduganova. We thank Gábor Danyi for help with the Hungarian texts.

In-person work and events were essential to this project, and we would have been unable to organize them without generous help from our partners. In Travneve, Ukraine, we thank the community and the Nazar Voitovych Art Residence and its director Lucy Nychai for generous and unstinting support of our summer institute, including the online symposia and the artists' retreat. In Lviv, we thank Ihor Petriy, Academic Secretary at the Scientific Library of Lviv National University, for planning assistance early in the project and essential logistical support in Lviv. We thank the staff and administration at the Scientific Library of Lviv National University for their generous support of our in-person symposia. Many inadequate thanks to Olena Kayinska and (again!) Lucy Nychai and the staff of

HallArtHall, Hnat Khotkevych Palace of Culture, for their care, companionship, administrative infrastructure, and artistic vision in support of the art exhibition and reading associated with the seminars.

Also in Lviv, we thank the very well-connected designer Dr. Demyan Voytovych, who teaches architecture at Lviv College of Decorative and Applied Arts in Ukraine and is a lecturer at Lviv Polytechnic National University. Early in the project, poet Kevin Vaughn and Antonia Szabari, associate professor of French and comparative literature at the University of Southern California, provided helpful advice and mentoring as we developed our ideas. Ostap Slyvynsky not only took part in the Lviv panel and contributed to this volume but provided guidance and advice from the earliest stages of the project. Dr. Sasha Dovzhyk helped us make important connections during a very busy time, and we thank her for her support. Małgorzata and Krzysztof Czyżewski from the Borderland Foundation in Poland dedicated time and energy to our project, and we extend our thanks for their help.

Our online conversations were particularly enlivened by journalist Janine di Giovanni (The Reckoning Project), Croatian writer Slavenka Drakulić, and poet and editor Diana Arterian. We thank Snezana Ung, Oksana Lutsyshyna, Kristina Hook, Daryna Gladun, and Lesyk Panasiuk for taking part in online panels. Professor Marci Shore and Professor Zsuzsa Selyem joined us in Lviv and made essential contributions to our conversations. Other invaluable panelists in Lviv include Professor Yaroslav Hrytsak of the Ukrainian Catholic University, editor in chief of the leading Ukrainian scholarly journal *Ukraina Moderna*; Danylo Ilnytskyi, literary critic, essayist, and senior lecturer at the Ukrainian Catholic University; and Yurko Prokhasko, Lviv National University lecturer, translator (from German, Polish and Yiddish), author, and psychoanalyst. Poet Iya Kiva gave a memorable reading of her poems at the art opening in Lviv. Additionally, we offer words of gratitude to Ukrainian poets who shared their testimonies with ariel rosé.

Our colleagues at the Universidad Autónoma de Baja California in Mexicali, Mexico, were generous with their time, participation, and ideas, and we thank Dr. Christian Alonso Fernandez Huerta in particular for moderating and organizing the guests. Dra. Liliana Lanz, Dr. Hugo Mendez Fierros, Dra. Lilian Paola Ovalle, and Dr. Fernando Vizcarra deepened our discussions before and during the panel.

We thank Occidental College, particularly Professor Damian Stocking and Romy Corona, for their support of Dr. Sushytska's online symposia in 2022. At the

University of Redlands, we are especially grateful to Sara Thompson, Katie Milsom, Professor Graeme Auton, Professor Steven Moore, Associate Provost Anne Cavender, College of Arts and Sciences Dean Justin Rose, Wendy Everhart, and the staff of Accounts Payable who manage our grant. Thanks to James Cole for video editing, and the University of Redlands Office of Community Service Learning and Engagement for supporting his internship.

On a more intimate note, we thank our hosts and family, helpers and supporters: Les Canterbury, Patricia Slaughter, Alina Sushytska, Volodymyr Bordyuk, Vatche and Gaia Sahakian, and Lauren Dubowski.

For necessary sustenance, thanks to Code Coffee, Cafe Veronika, Swit Kavy, Kupol, and the lively streets of Lviv.

***

Andriy Sodomora's "The Flute" originally appeared in Andriy Sodomora, *Sliozy rechei: Novely, obrazky, medytatsii* [The tears of things: Novellas, sketches, meditations] (Lviv: Piramida, 2010).

Andriy Sodomora's "The Dance" appeared in *Usmikh rechei: Etiudy, obrazky, novely, essei* [The smiles of things: Vignettes, sketches, novellas, essays] (Lviv: Piramida, 2017).

The English versions of the two stories by Andriy Sodomora are excerpted from The Tears and Smiles of Things (Boston: Academic Studies Press, 2024), translated by Roman Ivashkiv and Sabrina Jaszi.

An English version of Andrei Krasniashchikh's "Nadezhda; or, Hope," appeared in *Eurozine*, September 15, 2023.

Maša Kolanović's "Wartime Necessities" is excerpted from *Sloboština Barbie* (Zagreb: VBZ, 2008) and the English translation *Underground Barbie* (Chicago: Sandorf Passage, 2025) by Ena Selimović.

A version of Ihor Pomerantsev's "Humanitarian Corridor" appeared in his book: Igor Pomerantsev, *Moe pervoe bomboubezhyshche* [My first bomb shelter] (Kyiv: Drukarskii dvor, 2024). Portions of the essay appeared in English in a different version, translated by Frank Williams, as "Death is a Master from Russia," *Oxonian Review*, August 9, 2022.

The German translations of Miglena Nikolchina's poems previously appeared in *Neue Literature*, special edition dedicated to Bulgarian literature presented at the Leipzig Book Fair, Spring 1999.

Iya Kiva's poems appear in Ukrainian in *Smikh zgasloi vatry* [Laughter of an extinguished fire] (Kyiv: Dukh i litera, 2023). The English translations previously appeared in *Cafe Review*, Summer 2024.

Marianna Gyurász's "Február huszonnégy" was published in a special issue of *Kalligram* 7–8 (2022), published in response to the invasion of Ukraine. A PDF of the issue can be found here: https://tinyurl.com/e454fm7e.

ariel rosé's essay "Ukraine—A Polyphony" appeared in Finnish translation in *Särö* (October 2024), https://sarolehti.net/lehti/monien-aanien-ukraina, in Norwegian translation in Vinduet (October 2023), https://tinyurl.com/5d2cv3ty, in English translation in *Asymptote Journal* (October 2024), https://www.asymptotejournal.com/nonfiction/ariel-rose-ukraine-a-polyphony, and in French translation in *En Attendant Nadeau* (November 2023), https://www.en-attendant-nadeau.fr/2022/11/23/ukraine-concert-voix/.

Contributors

Céline Anger is an independent scholar and translator based in Paris, France.

Gassia Artin was born in Beirut, Lebanon. She holds a PhD in Near Eastern archaeology from the University of Lyon, France. She is currently a research affiliate at the Archéorient Maison de l'Orient et de la Méditerranée (CNRS), an assistant professor at the Lebanese University, and a cultural mediator for the Arab World Institute in Paris. Her creative endeavors include poetry, calligraphy, and painting.

Jessica Berlin is a political analyst, senior fellow at the Center for European Policy Analysis (CEPA), founder of the strategy consultancy CoStruct, a board member of the fintech company Bridge Technologies, and a board member of the German-Ukrainian Society. She has over seventeen years' experience in security, foreign policy, and economic partnership development in Africa, Asia, Europe, the Middle East, and North America, including with the US Senate, US Department of Defense, the German Aid Agency, and as a consultant to public, private, and nonprofit organizations. Berlin's commentary has been featured on CNN, the BBC, the *Washington Post*, NPR, *DW News*, *Le Monde*, ZDF, *Tagesspiegel*, and NZZ. She holds an MSc in the political economy of emerging markets from King's College London, a BA in international relations from Tufts University, and speaks five languages.

Uilleam Blacker is associate professor in Ukrainian and East European culture in the School of Slavonic and East European Studies, University College, London. A widely published scholar and translator specializing in Ukrainian and East-Central European literature and culture, he has written for the *Atlantic*, the *Guardian*, and the *TLS*, and commented on Ukrainian culture, history, and politics for the BBC, the *Guardian*, the *Telegraph*, Al Jazeera, ITV, and many more. His translations of Ukrainian authors have been published in the *Guardian*, the *White Review*, *Modern Poetry in Translation*, *Words without Borders*, and more. He was a judge for the International Booker Prize and, in 2022, he was the Paul Celan translation fellow at the Institute for Human Sciences, Vienna. Before joining UCL SSEES as a lecturer in 2014, he held postdoctoral positions at the universities of Oxford and Cambridge; prior to that, he studied at UCL SSEES, the Jagiellonian University in Kraków, and at the University of Glasgow. He has held research fellowships from the British Academy, the Leverhulme Foundation, and the Arts and Humanities Research Council.

Literary historian **Gábor Danyi**'s research focuses on cultural resistance in Hungary during the Cold War, with a special emphasis on unofficial publications. After many years of research, his monograph on the history of samizdat in Hungary between 1956 and 1989 was published in Hungarian in 2023. He also works as a literary translator, translating mainly Polish contemporary prose into Hungarian.

Marianna Gyurász was born in Komárom, Slovakia, in 1991. She graduated in molecular biology from Comenius University in Bratislava, and currently lives in Budapest. She writes poetry and prose in Hungarian. Her first book of poetry was published in 2022 by Kalligram, entitled *Már nem a mi völgyünk* (No longer our valley).

Garrett Howard is a student of comparative studies in literature and culture at Occidental College in California. He is interested in Russian and Serbo-Croatian literature, culture, and translation.

Translator **Roman Ivashkiv** is an Assistant Professor of Slavic Languages and Literatures at the University of Alabama. He has published extensively on translation studies and psycholinguistics.

Sabrina Jaszi is a translator from Uzbek, Russian, and Ukrainian based in California. She is the co-founder of the Turkolsavia translation collective and an editor of its journal *Turkoslavia*. Her published translations include the fiction of Salomat Vafo, O'tkir Hoshimov, Suhbat Aflatuni, Semyon Lipkin, and Reed

Grachev. With Roman Ivashkiv she translated Andriy Sodomora's *The Tears and Smiles of Things* (Academic Studies Press, 2024).

Iya Kiva is a Ukrainian poet, translator, and member of Pen Ukraine. She was born in 1984 in Donetsk and studied philology and cultural studies at Donetsk National University. In 2014 she was forced to move to Kyiv because of the Russo-Ukrainian War and is now based in Lviv. She is the author of three poetry collections: *Podal'she ot raia* «Подальше от рая» (Futher from Heaven, 2018), *Persha storinka zymy* «Перша сторінка зими» (The first page of winter, 2019), *Smikh zgasloi vatry* «Сміх згаслої ватри» (Laughter of an extinguished fire, 2023), as well as a book of interviews with Belarusian authors *My prokynemos' inshymy: Rozmovy z sychasnymy bilorus'kymy pys'mennykamy pro mynule, teperishnie i maibutnie Bilorusi* «Ми прокинемось іншими: розмови з сучасними білоруськими письменниками про минуле, теперішнє і майбутнє Білорусі» (We'll wake up different: Conversations with contemporary Belarusian writers on the past, present, and future of Belarus, 2021), dedicated to the 2020–2021 protests in Belarus. Kiva's poems have been translated into more than thirty languages. Her poetry books in translations have been published in Bulgaria, Poland, Italy, and Sweden. She is a winner of the Second Poetic Tournament Named after Nestor the Chronicler (2019), laureate of the Special Prize "LitAkcent" Award (2019) for her book *Persha storinka zymy*, laureate of the Literature Prize "Metaphor" for translators (2020), and more. She was also on the short list of the Women in Arts Award, "The Resistance 2024," founded by the Ukrainian Institute and UN Women Ukraine. She has participated in numerous writers' residencies and fellowship programs; for example, the Gaude Polonia Fellowship Program of the Minister of Culture of Poland (2021) and the International Writing Program (2023, USA).

Maša Kolanović is a prize-winning author and scholar best known for her genre-bending fiction and poetry. Her books include the poetry collection *Pijavice za usamljene* (Leeches for the lonely, 2001), the novel *Sloboština Barbie* (Underground Barbie, 2008), the prose poem *Jamerika* (2013), and the short story collection *Poštovani kukci i druge jezive price* (Dear pests and other creepy stories, 2019). The latter received the 2020 EU Prize for Literature, the Pula Book Fair Audience Award, and the Vladimir Nazor Prize for Literature. She is an associate professor in the Department of Croatian Studies at the University of Zagreb.

Marcell Komor is a Hungarian writer. He likes pseudonyms and conceptual word games. In the Hungarian language *komor* means "gloomy," "dark."

Ukrainian writer **Andrei Krasniashchikh** was born in 1970 in Poltava. He lives in Kharkiv where he is an associate professor in the Department of the History of Foreign Literature and Classical Philology at Karazin National University, and co-founder and co-editor of the literature magazine SP. He contributes to the Ukrainian online media outlet *Ukrainska Pravda* and his short stories have been widely translated and published in literary journals worldwide. He has received several awards, including the 2002 Laureate of the Ukrainian National Festival of Contemporary Art and the Kharkiv O. Maselsky Regional Literary Competition in multiple years. His book *Ukrainian Nostradamus* appeared in 2005, followed by several more books of criticism, literary biography, and short fiction and nonfiction, most recently *Kharkiv: As bombs fall and Poltava: Displaced persons* (2023).

Svetlana Lavochkina is a Ukrainian-born, internationally published novelist, poet, and literary translator. She has lived in Germany since 1999.

Andriy Lysenko was born in Crimea, Ukraine, and now lives in Lviv, Ukraine. An architect by training, he is a writer, translator, and literary editor.

Philip Nikolayev is a poet living in Boston. He translates poetry from several languages, with a current focus on Ukraine. His work has been published internationally, in such periodicals as *Poetry*, the *Paris Review*, the *Harvard Review*, and *Grand Street*. His several collections of verse include *Monkey Time* (Wave Books; winner of the 2001 Verse Prize) and *Letters from Aldenderry* (Salt). He is co-editor in chief of *Fulcrum: An Anthology of Poetry and Aesthetics*.

Miglena Nikolchina is a Bulgarian poet, writer, and theoretician whose research interests involve the interactions of literature and philosophy. Her poems and short stories have appeared in various languages. In English, her publications include numerous articles as well as the books *Matricide in Language: Writing Theory in Kristeva and Woolf* (2004) and *Lost Unicorns of the Velvet Revolutions: Heterotopias of the Seminar* (2013). Her most recent books (in Bulgarian) are *God with Machine: Subtracting the Human* (2022) and the collective volume *Video Games: The Dangerous Muse* (2023).

Oleh Panasiuk is a painter, graphic artist, and book illustrator who lives and works in Volhynia, Ukraine. He studied printmaking and book design at the Ukrainian Academy of Printing in Lviv.

Ihor Pomerantsev was born in Saratov, USSR, in 1948. He studied English philology and pedagogy at the University of Chernivtsy (Czernowitz). His poetry was first published in 1972 in the Moscow magazine *Smena*. At this time he also became involved with the Ukrainian civil rights movement. In 1979 he moved to London to work for the BBC Russian Service. In 1987 he moved to Munich to produce the Russian-language culture program *Over the Barriers* for Radio Free Europe/Radio Liberty, which he continues to do to this day. Pomerantsev has lived in Prague since 1995. His contributions—translated into German and/or English—created the impetus and the editorial basis for the digital time train Zeitzug, online since 2008. Starting in 2010 he became one of the founding members of the International Poetry Festival Meridian in Czernowitz. He is the author of a dozen poetry, fiction, and nonfiction books. His poetry collections have been translated into Ukrainian, Czech, Polish, English, German, and other languages.

ariel rosé (they/them) is a poet, illustrator, essayist, and translator, originally from Poland, resident of Norway, currently a nomad. They are the author of the poetry book with illustrations *Północ Przypowieści* (North parables), published by Znak in 2019, nominated for the Polish-German Josepha Award, and *morze nocą jest mięśniem serca* (the sea at night is a muscle of the heart), published by PIW in 2022, nominated for the Orfeusz Award. For their illustrations to Magdalena Tulli's book *Ten i tamten las* (Wilk & Król, 2017) they received the Warsaw Literary Award and were nominated for the International IBBY Award. They are a member of the Literary Union, the Association of Literary Translators in Poland, Circolo Scandinavo in Rome, and Litteratur på Blå in Oslo, where they invite poets from marginalized countries. They have two essay books forthcoming: *Ukraine—A Polyphony* and *Ways of Swimming*. Their portfolio can be accessed at: https://www.arielrose.art/.

Marco Schindelmann's affiliations, activities, and grants include: the University of Redlands (professor emeritus); the Arts Council for the City of Long Beach; Bayerische Staatsoper, Munich; NPR; the Dung Mummy Festival; SIGGRAPH; the Los Angeles Municpal Art Gallery; Galerjia '73 Belgrad; CEMC/EMSAN, Beijing, China; the NUS Arts Festival, Singapore; the Hong Kong Arts Centre,

Teater Kecil Taman Ismail Marzuki, Jakarta, Indonesia; the Yogyakarta Contemporary Music Festival; *Computer Music Journal* (MIT); Centaur Records; New World Records; the Los Angeles Music Center; the NEA; and the American Geo-Spatial Agency.

Ena Selimović is a Yugoslav-born writer and co-founder of Turkoslavia, a translation collective and journal. Her work has appeared in the *Periodical of the Modern Language Association, Words without Borders,* the *Los Angeles Review of Books, World Literature Today,* and elsewhere, and has received support from the American Literary Translators Association, the American Council of Learned Societies, and the National Endowment for the Arts. She holds a PhD in comparative literature from Washington University in St. Louis.

Zsuzsa Selyem is a novelist and works as associate professor of contemporary literature at Babes-Bolyai University, Cluj, Romania. One of the most experimental voices in mid-generation Hungarian fiction, she has published two volumes of short stories, two novels, and five volumes of essays to date. *It's Raining in Moscow* (Contra Mundum Press), translated by Erika Mihálycsa and Peter Sherwood, appeared in 2020, and it was among the most notable translations of the year, according to *World Literature Today.*

Marci Shore is professor of history at Yale University and a regular visiting fellow at the Institut für die Wissenschaften vom Menschen in Vienna. Her research focuses on the intellectual history of twentieth- and twenty-first-century Central and Eastern Europe. She is the translator of Michał Głowiński's *The Black Seasons* and the author of *Caviar and Ashes: A Warsaw Generation's Life and Death in Marxism, 1918–1968, The Taste of Ashes: The Afterlife of Totalitarianism in Eastern Europe.* A new edition of her third book, *The Ukrainian Night: An Intimate History of Revolution,* was published in March 2024. Her articles and essays have appeared in the *New Yorker, Foreign Policy, Eurozine,* the *Atlantic,* the *New York Review of Books,* the *Times Literary Supplement,* the *New York Times,* and the *Wall Street Journal.* In 2018 she received a Guggenheim Fellowship for the book project she is currently completing about phenomenology in East-Central Europe tentatively titled *In Pursuit of Certainty Lost: Central European Encounters on the Way to Truth.*

Alisa Slaughter's essays, short fiction, and translations have appeared most recently in Flyway, terrain.org, and the *Santa Monica Review.* She co-translated *A Spy for an Unknown Country: Lectures and Essays by Merab Mamardashvili* (ibidem, 2020), and her collection of short fiction *Bad Habitats* was published in 2013 by Gold Line Press. She holds an MFA from Warren Wilson College and an MA in comparative literature from the University of Arizona, and teaches at the University of Redlands in California.

Ostap Slyvynsky is a Ukrainian poet, translator, essayist, and scholar. He has authored five books of poetry in Ukrainian, as well as *The Ukrainian Dictionary of War* (Lost Horse Press, 2024, translated by Grace Mahoney and Taras Malkovych). His poetry collections have been published in Germany, Poland, Czech Republic, Bulgaria, Macedonia, and Russia. He was the first program director of the International Literary Festival in Lviv in 2006–2007. In 2016–2018, he organized the literary project Literature against Aggression and the public discussion platform Stories of Otherness, a series of public interviews with writers, intellectuals, and civic activists who have suffered from different kinds of social exclusion. Since 2021, he has organized PEN Ukraine's festival Propysy (Writings) for novice authors. He was elected the vice president of PEN Ukraine in 2022. His main research interests are intercultural communication, the comparative history of the literatures of East-Central Europe, and the role of literature and popular culture in the construction of historical memory. In 2007, he earned a PhD degree in humanities. He is a frequent visiting lecturer at various Polish, Bulgarian, and Western European universities.

Born in 1937, **Andriy Sodomora** graduated from the Ivan Franko University of Lviv where he is currently professor of classics in the Department of Classical Philology. In 1962, the twenty-five-year-old Sodomora produced a Ukrainian translation of Menander's *Dyskolos,* a play whose original manuscript was recovered only in 1952. It was the first translation of this comedy in the Soviet Union, and since then Sodomora has served tirelessly as the Ukrainian "voice" of classical antiquity. Today, his translation oeuvre includes more than twenty-two translated volumes from ancient Greek and Roman authors, including Horace, Ovid, Lucretius, Sophocles, Aeschylus, Euripides, Seneca, Boethius, Cato the Elder,

Virgil, Sappho, Alcaeus of Mytilene, and Archilochus. In addition to his translations, Sodomora is well known for his literary studies, essays, and creative nonfiction. In the last decade, he has produced several books of poetry and short fiction. He is the winner of the BBC Ukraine Book of the Year Award, the UNESCO City of Literature Award, and the Antonovych Prize, among other accolades. Since the beginning of the war in Ukraine, Sodomora has been writing topical commentary that applies his vast knowledge of classical literature and philosophy to current affairs.

Julia Sushytska (PhD, philosophy, SUNY Stony Brook) teaches at Occidental College. She co-translated and edited *A Spy for an Unknown Country: Lectures and Essays by Merab Mamardashvili* (ibidem, 2020). Her articles have appeared in peer-reviewed journals (*Mosaic, Angelaki, Philosophy Today,* the *Journal of Aesthetic Education, Tapuya, Eidos, Janus Unbound*) and edited volumes (*Rethinking Mamardashvili, Gilles Deleuze and Metaphysics* and *Philosophy, Society and the Cunning of History in Eastern Europe*). Among her recent publications are "Becoming Homeless in Language: On Ontological Terrorism" (*Janus Unbound*), "The Illusion of a Crossroads: Parmenides, Arendt, Mamardashvili and the Space for Truth" (*Eidos*), and "Metics and the Art of Playing with Contradictions" (*Tapuya*).

Since 1994, **Gabriele Tiemann** has been translating Bulgarian literature, including poetry, cultural studies, films, and art projects. She holds a PhD in Slavonic (Bulgarian) literary studies, and teaches literature, language, and translation seminars in German and Bulgarian universities. She divides her time between Germany and Bulgaria.

Frank L. Vigoda is the pen name for the Polish-English literary translation partnership of Ann Frenkel and Gwido Zlatkes. Their translations have appeared in the *New York Review of Books,* the *Boston Review, Lyric Poetry Review,* and *Modern Poetry in Translation,* among other journals. In 2025 World Poetry Books will publish a collection of poems by Witold Wirpsza in their translation. Two other recent translations are the autobiography of Karol Modzelewski, *Riding History to Death* (Rowman & Littlefield, 2021), and *Against the Devil in History: Poems, Short Stories, Essays, Fragments,* by Aleksander Wat (Slavica Publishers, 2018). They have also translated a collection of poems by ariel rosé.

Serhiy Zhadan, poet, novelist, essayist, and translator, was born in 1974 in Starobilsk, a town in the east of Ukraine. He received a graduate degree in philology from Kharkiv University, where he then taught Ukrainian and world literature. Since 2004 he has been an independent writer. He performs with the ska band Sobaky v Kosmosi (Dogs in Space) and has released several albums, including the 2014 *Byisia za nei* (Fight for her). Zhadan was an activist in the country's Orange (2004) and Maidan (2014) revolutions. His publications include *Mesopotamia* (2014), awarded the Angelus literature prize in 2015; *Voroshilovgrad* (2010), for which he received the 2014 Jan Michalski Prize for Literature and the BBC Ukrainian Book of the Decade award; and *Capital* (2006), which received both the Ukrainian Book of the Year award and the BBC Ukrainian Book of the Year award. His novel *Depeche Mode* (2004) was published in English by Glagoslav Publications in 2014. Zhadan's work has been translated into Russian, Polish, German, Czech, Belorussian, Latvian, Italian, Hungarian, English, and French.

www.ingramcontent.com/pod-product-compliance
Lightning Source LLC
LaVergne TN
LVHW072315010825
817679LV00052B/1496

* 9 7 9 8 8 9 7 8 3 0 2 9 9 *